Lesbian and Bisexual Identities

Lesbian and Bisexual Identities

Constructing Communities,
Constructing Selves

KRISTIN G. ESTERBERG

TEMPLE UNIVERSITY PRESS
Philadelphia

Temple University Press, Philadelphia 19122
Copyright © 1997 by Kristin G. Esterberg
Published 1997
Printed in the United States of America

⊗ The paper used in this publication meets the requirements of
American National Standards for Information Sciences—Permanence
of Paper for Printed Library Materials, ANSI Z39.48-1984

Text design by Kate Nichols

Library of Congress Cataloging-in-Publication Data

Esterberg, Kristin G.
    Lesbian and bisexual identities : constructing communities,
constructing selves / Kristin G. Esterberg.
        p.   cm.
    Includes bibliographical references and index.
    ISBN 1-56639-509-7 (cloth : alk. paper). — ISBN 1-56639-510-0
(paper : alk. paper)
    1. Lesbians—Identity.   2. Lesbians—Social conditions.
3. Bisexual women.   4. Lesbian communities.   I. Title.
HQ75.5E85   1997
305.9′06643—dc20   96-35409

For Sue and Katherine

Contents

Acknowledgments

I am grateful to a number of people for help, advice, criticism, and playful diversions while writing this book. Although this book is not at all a warmed-over version of my dissertation, I wish to thank first of all my doctoral committee at Cornell University. Phyllis Moen has continued to be a supportive mentor, both in and out of graduate school. I am grateful for her advice and encouragement. Ritch C. Savin-Williams encouraged me to write about lesbian issues early on, and he continues to do so. Lynn Smith-Lovin sparked my interest in identity.

Kay Forest at Northern Illinois University, Ellen Bradburn, and Jeff Longhofer at the University of Missouri–Kansas City (UMKC) have provided critical companionship, for which I am most appreciative. Two students at UMKC, Tobie Matava and Jennifer Watts, have indulged me in long, rambling conversations about lesbian identity and lesbian community. Becky Major has been a most capable research assistant, miraculously appearing when I most needed her.

Several people have provided critical feedback on parts of the manuscript. Steve Seidman's comments on Chapter 4 were invaluable. On long trips to the Immigration Service and on other occasions, Sue Bergmeier gave gentle feedback on early drafts of Chapter 5 and other sections of the book. The Women's Studies Consortium of Kansas City provided a forum to read and critique parts of the manuscript. Mike Ames has been a superlative editor, encouraging me to delete countless pages. Katie Ren Peng Bergmeier has been an admirable diversion, crumpling discarded manuscript pages with undisguised glee and cheering me up when I was faced with the task of revising.

A number of individuals and institutions have supported this work financially. A Beatrice Brown award from the Women's Studies program at Cornell University enabled me to conduct the first taped interviews, and an award from the Department of Manuscripts and Archives at Cornell University provided funds to transcribe the first set of interview tapes. I am especially grateful to Brenda Marston, Human Sexuality Archivist, and Tom Hickerson, Director of Rare and Manuscript Collections, for those funds. Brenda's friendship sustained me through much of the data collection. A faculty research grant from the University of Missouri–Kansas City provided funding for conducting the reinterviews in 1995. The Sociology Department at UMKC graciously granted me a one-semester leave to focus exclusively on my writing.

Two running buddies in Kansas City, LaVerne and Jan, have helped me keep sane while writing this manuscript.

To my partner, Sue Bergmeier, I am deeply thankful. She makes life sweeter and more meaningful in uncountable ways.

Finally, to all of the women who patiently told me (and retold me) their stories, sorted cards, filled out questionnaires, referred their friends, and in general made this book possible, I thank you. Your stories have been an extraordinary gift.

Lesbian and Bisexual Identities

Introduction

Kate Foster, a white woman in her forties who grew up in the South, came out as a lesbian in the late 1960s, before the Stonewall Rebellion marked the birth of the gay liberation movement in 1969. She first suspected that she might be a lesbian in the late 1950s, when at age twelve she "had a mad crush on a woman who was thirteen years older than [she] was." As Kate recalled, "It seemed to be out of proportion to what I was supposed to be feeling about anybody other than boys my age."

Despite the persistence of these strong feelings for women, Kate did not consider herself a lesbian until much later. "I made a pact with Jesus at the time," she said. "I was from a very religious family, and we went to church three times a week, and this woman happened to be in the church choir. So this one particular day when I was very obsessed with my potential perversion, I was waiting until the church service began. And I started praying, and I said, 'Dear God. If I'm queer, give me a sign.' Of course, I picked the sign, and that sign was that G. would not appear in the choir that Sunday morning. Well, it was pretty easy to get my wish, my confirmation of my normative status, because G. appeared in the choir every Sunday morning almost with the regularity of the sun coming up. So it wasn't exactly like asking wine to come from the rock. Nevertheless, she walked in. I felt relieved, and I didn't think about the issue again until I was eighteen."

At age eighteen she found herself "passionately kissing another woman": "It occurred to me that the problem had not entirely been resolved. . . . And my reaction to that first encounter, that passionate kiss, was to get up out of bed, brush my teeth vigorously, walk back to the bed, and say, 'I'm not that kind of girl.' And the next night I was that kind of girl all over again!"

"Between the ages of nineteen and twenty there was a year-and-a-half to two-year period in which I was quite convinced that my affair with M. had been just a mistake, one of those biological bleeps that occur. I did not doubt that I was heterosexual and felt that I simply, for whatever reason, had gotten my sexual orientation slightly confused. I did not at that time discredit my feelings about M., but was convinced that once she was gone and I was over that breakup that I would pick up and go on my merry heterosexual way, which I proceeded to do. It was only when I realized that I was attracted to women other than M. that I could no longer ignore the fact that I was in fact probably predominantly attracted to women. . . . And from that point on with rare exception I considered myself homosexual."

When Kate became involved with feminism, her interpretation of her sexual identity began to change. "Up until 1975, I described myself as gay. And when I began to understand the political significance of my sexual preference and my choice to be exclusively homosexual, I began to use the term lesbian. Because for me it described not only my private life but my stance in the world and how I viewed . . . my life as a type of social critique." Kate said, "As a lesbian, I was not in any way having to either at an economic level or a social level or psychological level put myself in a position of subordination to a male relationship."

Looking back, Kate says, "I had some encounters with men that made me believe that in a different society I would perhaps be bisexual. However, I didn't [make that choice], because I felt there was something fundamentally a part of my essence that I had to honor, in my own psychological health. Socially, I could have been heterosexual. Psychologically, I think I have always been homosexual. I've always been a lesbian. . . . And at this point in my life, my lesbian identity is absolutely clear. It's as much a part of me as having brown eyes."

Kate's story documents just one of the ways in which women may arrive at a lesbian or bisexual identity. There are many other identity accounts. Some see their sexual identities as basic, fixed, not open to change or reinterpretation; whereas others see their identities as essentially fluid, changing over the life course in response to changing contexts and circumstances. Some see their identities as something unwelcome, painfully acknowledged, and only with great difficulty transformed into a source of pride. Yet others see their identity as a gift or blessing, and a source of great joy.

Although nearly five years older, Joan Borman, a Jewish feminist, came to define herself as a lesbian over ten years after Kate had. Joan recounted, "I got married as soon as I graduated from college, and I had been married for eleven years. And then I left my husband, my former husband, for another man. I fell in love with another man, . . . and I lived with him for almost five years. And then I decided to leave him and be on my own. . . . But I think that part of the process of leaving him was a recognition that I wasn't going to be with any other men in my life. That I had no desire to be with another man in my life." This led her toward a lesbian identity: "There have certainly been times in my life that I have been celibate, but since I understood that I was going to be a sexual person, and since I was very serious about not being involved with men, it seemed that there was nothing else. There was only one alternative."

For Joan, who had long been involved in progressive politics, coming out as a lesbian was not a decision about her sexual self: "I didn't come out because I had always been miserable as a straight woman, as far as sex was concerned. I had always been miserable as a straight woman as far as emotion was concerned, and so it was very hard, sort of testing out the lesbian world. . . . There were times when my sexual relationships with women were either not as satisfying or differently satisfying, and so it took quite a while for me to sort through that. . . . I was not someone who spent all of my life thinking 'I really must be a lesbian and what am I going to do with this.' But [I] saw it as an opening up of possibilities for my life, and the reason that I saw that is because other women had created a world that I could see."

Joan's lesbian identity is clearly related to her feminism, her progressive politics, and the visible lesbian culture and community that women had begun to create in the 1970s. Her identity account seems clearly rooted in choice. Yet in reflecting on the years that she has lived as a lesbian, she has come to a somewhat different understanding. When she came out in the early 1980s, she said, "I felt at the time as if I were making a choice. On the other hand, I felt as if I couldn't continue to live the life that I had been living—the straight life. I couldn't do that anymore. The more that I knew, the more that I questioned, the more that I read, the less palatable it was for me, the less I could find ways of pretending to myself that I was enjoying what was going on. . . . Now when I look back on it, I sort of see this inexorable pull toward something that I now define as a lesbian existence, because what's clear to me now is that whatever the ups and downs of daily life, whatever the problems, . . . I am not crazy the way I was when I was straight."

Kate's and Joan's stories represent only two of the identity accounts women offer. This book focuses on the variety of stories lesbian and bisexual women tell about who they are and the community they live in. An open lesbian, I lived in a small eastern community from 1986 to 1991. From 1988 to 1991, I conducted interviews and surveys with approximately 120 lesbian and bisexual women in this community. In 1994, I returned to see how the community had changed, to reinterview some of the original women, and to conduct new interviews. Based on the interviews and my experiences in the community, this book examines the stories lesbian and bisexual women tell about who they are, how they come to see themselves as lesbian or bisexual, and what those identities mean to them. Yet identities are not constructed in isolation. Their meanings arise in part from the social and historical contexts in which people find themselves. This book thus examines as well the community in which these women live. In interviews and surveys, women describe "the" lesbian community they live in: how they see its structure, its social groups, its informal rules and norms for behavior, and their places inside—or on the margins of—the community.

Although technically a city, this community has the flavor of a cosmopolitan small town. Despite a relatively small population (less than 35,000), the city, like many other college towns, supports numerous environmental, political, and social groups; food cooperatives and credit unions; and an array of bookstores, movie houses, restaurants, and small businesses. The city tends to elect more progressive politicians and to enact more progressive legislation than many other cities of its size and location. In 1984, for example, the city passed a fair practice ordinance prohibiting discrimination on the basis of sexual orientation, and, in 1990, the city passed a domestic partnership ordinance, which allows lesbian and gay couples (as well as unmarried heterosexual couples) to register their partnerships and gain access to some of the privileges accorded to married heterosexual couples. For these reasons, the city attracts a fairly large lesbian and gay population.

The community has many resources for lesbians and gays (and far fewer for bisexuals). It supports a number of political organizations, support groups, businesses, a mixed lesbian and gay bar, and a women's book store. The Lesbian and Gay Task Force (which changed its name in the early 1990s to the Lesbian, Gay, and Bisexual Task Force) holds monthly meetings and sponsors coffeehouses, concerts, lectures, and other social events. For a brief time, branches of Act Up and Queer Nation, both dedicated to direct-action politics, were active. Lesbian and bisexual women are active in the Task Force and other organizations. They gather socially in a number of places: at the bar, at concerts produced by a women's music production company, at softball games during the summer, at card games, and at private parties.

Over the period of the study, the lesbian community had changed relatively little. New women moved into town and others moved away; some groups folded and others became larger and stronger. Over the six-year period, a lesbian "baby boom" became very much in evidence. A number of women gave birth to children or adopted, and a mothers' support group was started. Ideologically, the community seemed to become looser, a little more tolerant. Yet in key ways, the community seemed much the same. There were still fairly deep divisions between those who were associated with the university and college and those who lived downtown. The Task Force was still the center of lesbian/gay political life downtown, while those who were involved in women's studies, in one way or another, were at the heart of lesbian life on campus. Although there was, increasingly, crossover between the two groups, many long-time residents were suspicious of students and other transient residents.

Lesbian communities are not constructed unproblematically; nor are they monolithic. For some women, especially bisexual women, lesbian community is a painful myth. Faced with rejection or demands for conformity from those whom they feel should be most accepting, some lesbians and bisexual women have abandoned the notion of community. Yet others see lesbian community as a lifeline and source of camaraderie. Some drift in and out of the community, at times pushing to be near the "center," and at other times drawing back. Highlighting the stories of all three groups of women, this book explores both sides of lesbian and bisexual community life.

Presenting the women's accounts in their own words is a major emphasis of this book. But the book also attempts to move beyond storytelling, seeking to understand how these women's accounts of their lives resonate with social science theories of identity and community. Much theorizing about lesbian and gay identity takes place outside the realm of empirical research, and up until very recently, little attention has been paid to bisexuality.[1] Few have attempted to explore lesbian and bisexual identities simultaneously. This book seeks to do both.

Drawing loosely on social constructionist approaches to identity, the book argues that identities are multiple and contingent. Created within the context of specific communities and within specific relationships, identities are ways of sorting through experiences of desires and attractions, relationships, and politics. And their meanings change over time: as women grow older and have more varied experiences, as their communities and sociopolitical environments change, and as life circumstances alter.

The women whose narratives are presented in this book understand their attractions to women—and to men—differently, depending on their own life situations and on the discourses about sexuality and sexual identity available to them. They used a variety of words and images to describe themselves, and these changed over time as they came to understand their sexual histories in different lights. In sharp contrast to the 1950s and early 1960s, the growth of a women's movement in the late 1960s and 1970s allowed women to claim explicitly feminist lesbian identities. As Kate clearly recognized, the lesbian feminism that she claimed in the mid 1970s was simply not possible when she first came out in the late 1960s. Similarly, Joan felt she simply would not have come out were it not for the feminist movement. And some years later, when Marcela Reyes, a young Latina lesbian, began to embrace the word *dyke* to describe herself, she did this as a conscious reclamation enabled by feminists and sex radicals writing and organizing in the 1980s.

Not all of the women interviewed saw their sexuality as an outgrowth of their feminism or changed their understandings of their sexuality in response to a feminist movement. Bonita Brown, an African American graduate student from a working-class background, grew up in a major urban area during the height of the women's movement. Yet her coming out was marked by isolation, fear, and loneliness. "I had read lesbian books and literature, but I had no idea that other lesbians existed. For some reason it did not click to me that if someone's writing these books, then there are other people like me." Meeting women was difficult "because I wouldn't identify myself. Because I wouldn't know how—I didn't even know how to go about it." Whether her isolation from feminism and other lesbians was due to the movement's seeming irrelevance to poor and working-class women and women of color, or to her own personal and family history, is not apparent. What *is* clear is that she did not experience the heady sense of liberation that some women expressed coming out as lesbians into a feminist movement and community.

As the women looked back during the interviews, they interpreted their histories through their present understandings of themselves. If interviewed at different points in time, the women may well have offered different life stories. This became particularly apparent when in 1994 I reinterviewed thirteen women who had initially been interviewed in 1989. For several, their accounts had changed dramatically. Perhaps most dramatic is Sally Zimmerman's story. At the first interview, she was working through the breakup of a long-term relationship with a woman and struggling to maintain the connection as their relationship changed. At that time, she felt herself to be strongly lesbian. At the time of the second interview, she was married to a man and still struggling to maintain connections with her former woman lover. But she did not feel herself to be heterosexual; nor did she feel strongly about the term bisexual. She felt, instead, like a lesbian involved with a man.

Changes in identity accounts such as these do not mean that Sally or any of the other women are on their way to discovering a "true" self: that their past accounts are somehow false or unreflective of who they "really" are and that the researcher, as privileged interpreter of their experiences, is the arbiter of the "true" meaning of those experiences. The interviewees' accounts do not tell us about some "objective" or reified process of coming to identify as lesbian or bisexual. But women's subjective understandings of their life histories are important in and of themselves, for these histories tell us how women, at least in one small community, over one period of time, came to situate themselves in a changing and complex social world.

How social science theories construct sexual identities is an important part of that landscape. These theories not only shape how researchers articulate the nature of sexual identity—even the notion that people *have* sexual identities—but they also determine what researchers see and hear when they solicit lesbians' and bisexuals' accounts. Through pop psychology and self-help books, such as JoAnn Loulan's popular series of books and lectures (1984, 1987), and through therapy and counseling, academic theories filter into lesbian and bisexual women's own accounts. Although this may be more the case in university communities and among those with higher levels of education, it also occurs more broadly.

For this reason, the book begins by examining social science theories of sexual identity. Over the last few decades, theory and research into the nature of identity has grown substantially. As

Philip Gleason (1983) documents, references to the concept were rare prior to the 1950s. Since that time, however, theories abound, not only in the fields of psychology and sociology but in literary theory, history, anthropology, and the growing field of queer theory. The term *identity* itself, as Gleason notes, is both "elusive and ubiquitous" (p. 910). Thus, a comprehensive review of the general literature on identity is well beyond the scope of this book. Even the literature on lesbian and gay identity is substantial. As Vivienne Cass characterized it in the early 1980s, the literature on homosexual identity is like "an overgrown garden, badly in need of pruning" (1983/1984, p. 106).

If the literature on lesbian/gay identity is an overgrown garden, then the literature on bisexual identity is a packet of seeds and an only partly sown field. Relatively few have conducted research into the nature of bisexual identity; and even fewer have attempted to theorize lesbian and bisexual identity simultaneously, without seeing bisexuality as lesser or merely a step along a lesbian path (Paula Rust [1992b, 1993] and Carla Golden [1994] are notable exceptions; see also Marjorie Garber [1995]). But bisexual women's identity accounts call into question the dual categories of sexuality created in modern Western societies. Although bisexuality has often been seen (at least by many lesbians and gay men) as a transitional stage prior to adopting a "true" lesbian or gay identity, for some women a lesbian identity is merely a transition point to a more stable sense of self as bisexual. The recent emergence of bisexual identity and, perhaps, a bisexual movement offers insight into the construction of sexual identities.

The first chapters of the book explore questions of sexual identity. Chapter 1 examines the social science literature on sexual identity, focusing on theories drawn from three major areas: developmental psychology, sociology, and, in a much more limited way, poststructuralism and queer theory. Throughout, theories of identity are grounded in women's accounts of their lives. Chapter

2 focuses more explicitly on the stories people tell to account for or explain their sexual identities. This chapter examines how women define their sexual identities, how they came to understand themselves as lesbian or bisexual, and so on. The identity accounts show that identities are not constructed in fixed, invariant ways; nor are they completely idiosyncratic. Using information from five-year follow-up interviews with thirteen women, Chapter 3 looks at some of the changes women experience over time. For some women, sexual identity is fluid. For others, sexual identity is more stable.

Chapter 4 focuses on lesbian style: the "performance" of lesbian identity and the shifting boundaries that interviewees drew between themselves and heterosexual women. This chapter examines how the women create a distinctive lesbian presence in the world, how they recognize others, and how their senses of what a lesbian "looks" like draw on and transform traditional formulations of masculinity and femininity.

Sexual identities may be among the most important identities individuals hold; yet they are certainly not the only identities. Although middle-class and white lesbians may not think of themselves as having specific race and class identities, race and class importantly shape individuals' life circumstances. Chapter 5 examines the multiple identities that lesbian and bisexual women hold, paying particular attention to race and class, and setting sexual identities within a larger social and political context.

Chapter 6 explores some of the historical and theoretical dimensions of lesbian/bisexual community and describes the somewhat contradictory meanings of community held by the women in this community. Instead of seeing community as a stable, geographically bounded entity, the chapter examines the meanings community holds for participants and the ways in which individuals fashion meaning out of a shared social category (di Leonardo 1984). Chapter 6 sets forth a notion of community as a set of overlapping friendship circles and explores the implications for women who are different.

Chapter 7 examines the rules for behavior—subtle and unspoken as well as more overt—that arose in this particular lesbian community. The chapter considers this paradox: How sometimes restrictive rules for behavior develop in a community based on principles of individual freedom and nonconformity to the mainstream society. Chapter 8 explores the variety of ways in which bisexual women define their sexuality, the difficulties in creating an autonomous bisexual community, and the limits to lesbian community posed by bisexual women. Yet not all lesbian and bisexual women experience their senses of themselves in the context of a community. Chapter 9 looks at the possibilities for creating identities outside the confines of a lesbian community. Some of the limits of community life are explored, and possibilities for reconceiving it in a less limiting way are offered.

1

Theorizing Identity

Lesbian and Bisexual Accounts

> I think when I started identifying myself as a lesbian it would have been when I was in my third year of college, maybe. Second year of college? Where I identified myself as that and felt good about it.
>
> DEBORAH SCHMIDT

> If lesbian means that you're not—haven't been in love with men, then, of course I am. But I mean mainly I've been in love with just one woman for a long, long time. So I guess I am.
>
> ANNE BIERSMITH

Anne and Deborah are friends. They are both about the same age, live in the same neighborhood, and grew up in the same conservative religious tradition. Yet they think of themselves in very different ways. For Deborah, it's important to identify herself, to label who she is, and to let others know about the various facets of her identity. Anne, on the other hand, resists labels. Although she knows how she feels, she gropes for a language to describe herself. Identities feel far too confining. They are just not that important to her.

People tell many different kinds of stories about who they are. Some think deeply about their identities and need to pin down and name exactly what and who they think they are. Others are more flexible, using identities more as a shorthand way to describe a process of coming to be. Despite the wide ranges of approaches to describing oneself, the use of identities to define who people are has proliferated in recent decades. Not surprisingly, academic literature on identities has proliferated in recent years as well.

Scholarship on identity has come from a variety of disciplines: from psychology (in both its clinical and academic versions), sociology, and the other social sciences to literary and cultural theory. In the four decades since the term has come into common parlance (Gleason 1983), it has taken on a variety of meanings. Morris Rosenberg (1987) has identified at least ten different meanings used by scholars, ranging from the sense of oneself as continuous, existing throughout time, to a sense of oneself as belonging to a group or having shared group membership. Some see identities as something essential, tangible, and real, inherent in the self; yet others see identities as shifting, constructed, a matter of creating meaning from social categories and coming to attach labels to oneself. The body of academic and popular literature on identity is so large that it nearly defies categorization. Perhaps no term has been used so much in recent years or become so popular—both in academic and in lay worlds—as identity.

Work on lesbian and gay identity is no exception. Since the 1970s, with the rise of a gay and lesbian liberation movement, speculation about the nature of sexual identity has flourished. With few exceptions, however, the literature on lesbian/gay identity has not directly referenced but has paralleled discussions of identity more generally (for exceptions, see Epstein 1987; Coyle 1992).

As historian Philip Gleason (1983) discusses, social science research into identity originated from two streams of thought: psychologist Erik Erikson's model of identity development (including the popularized notion of identity crisis) and a more sociological tradition, drawing on the work of role theorists and symbolic interactionists such as Erving Goffman and Anselm Strauss. In Erikson's model, identity development refers to the development of individual personality, a stable core sense of self, within the context of the social milieu in which the individual finds him or herself. Identity develops through the resolution of a series of tasks specific to each developmental stage. For Erikson and those following in his tradition, the notions of stability and interiority are key. That is, identity development is essentially an intrapsychic process, although occurring in the context of the social environment.

For sociologists, the emphasis is not on the interior life of the self but on the social components of identity and the possibilities of change. Identities are not something deep down inside the individual but are located in the interaction between the individual and society. Identities, thus, are always in process. For symbolic interactionists, identities refer to the names or labels that individuals attach to social positions (Stryker 1987, 1980; Burke and Franzoi 1988). They are the "meanings that one attributes to oneself as an object" (Burke and Tully 1977, p. 883), and they carry with them expectations for particular kinds of behaviors. Being a retail clerk carries different expectations for behavior than being a physician; being a daughter is different from being a sister. All of these identities require a social context: You cannot be a retail clerk if there is no store, no customers, or no goods to sell. You cannot be a sister without having someone to be a sister *to*.

The two conceptions of lesbian and gay identity dominant throughout the 1970s and early 1980s reflect these two ways of thinking about identity. One set of theories about lesbian and gay identity drew heavily on developmental psychology and the Eriksonian tradition (e.g., Cass 1979, 1983/1984; Minton and McDonald 1983/1984; Sophie 1985/1986; Troiden 1988; Gonsiorek and Rudolph 1991; Coleman 1982; Espín 1987). A second set drew more on labeling theories and symbolic interactionism (e.g., Plummer 1981; McIntosh 1981; Weeks 1981, 1987; Jenness 1992; Rust 1992a, 1992b, 1993; Simon and Gagnon 1967).

In recent years, postmodernism and an emerging queer theory have problematized the very notion of lesbian and gay identity (see, e.g., Warner 1993; de Lauretis 1991; Fuss 1991). Drawing heavily on the fields of literary theory and cultural studies, the new queer theory criticizes static notions of identity and identity-based politics. Focusing on flux and change, queer theory attempts to shift attention from "the politics of personal identity to the politics of signification" (Seidman 1993, p. 130). Rather than seeing lesbian and gay identities as something with a fixed and stable content, queer theory sees identities as fragmentary, partial, and shifting. For some, identities are performative, created by the interplay of mobile and shifting signs (Butler 1991). Queer theory draws attention to the exclusive and boundary-constructing nature of identification and encourages us to examine how the normalization of heterosexuality is caught up in attempts to construct lesbian and gay identities (Fuss 1991).

The Developmental Paradigm

Theorists who have drawn on developmental models typically see lesbian and gay identity as developing through a series of stages, beginning with a period of uncertainty about the self and one's sexuality and ending with a period of identity "integration" in which the individual embraces his or her lesbian/gay identity, sees it as being merely one facet of a complicated self, and becomes fully integrated into a heterosexual as well as a homosexual world.

Eli Coleman's (1982) model is fairly typical of stage models of identity development. He divides the developmental path into five stages: pre–coming out, in which individuals have only a "preconscious" awareness of a possible lesbian or gay identity; coming out, in which the individual begins to recognize and accept her or his sexual identity and tells another person about it; exploration, in which the individual makes contact with and explores the lesbian/gay community; first relationship, in which the individual grows comfortable with his or her identity and becomes involved with a same-gender partner; and integration, in which the individual becomes "fully functioning" within society.

Although the exact number, content, and endpoint of stages may differ, as well as the possibility for nonlinear movement among them, stage models all suffer from a number of defects. First, they assume a biologistic, static sense of sexual identity (Weinberg 1984; Kitzinger 1987). Identity is developed "once"; presumably, once an individual has reached the pinnacle of development, further change stops. Alternative routes to the same identity or changes in identity (e.g., a shift from a lesbian to bisexual identity) remain untheorized by the stage models; at most, deviations from the ideal-typical model are seen as regressions, *deviations* from the developmental path. Some have argued that the stage models are built on a male model, reflecting men's experiences more than women's (Faderman 1985). Women's sexuality, they argue, is more fluid and changeable than men's. Thus, in the developmental schema women are seen as immature, unintegrated. Other critics argue that holding rigid identities may indicate an inability to adapt to changing circumstances. In a fast moving world, Paula Rust (1993) notes, individuals may respond to new social conditions (such as the increasing acceptance of bisexuality) by changing their sexual identities. These shifts may well be a sign of flexibility and psychological health, not immaturity.

Although a number of theorists have provided empirical tests of stage models (Sophie 1985/1986; Cass 1983/1984), these models simply do not reflect the enormous variation in women's stories. Wendy Hammond's account, for instance, seems consistent with stage models of sexual identity development. A professional woman in her late thirties, Wendy began to consider that she might be lesbian in her early adolescence. "I had a . . . tremendous amount of anxiety about something being wrong with me and started to focus in on my sexual identity." After a number of years in which she fought her attractions to women, she slowly began to accept herself. "I was very homophobic, ashamed of the thought of being gay, and feeling that certainly this couldn't be a possibility. There was a little bit of a war going on in my head." It was not until she was in her late twenties, when she was involved in a long-term relationship with a woman, her second lover, that she began to feel comfortable telling others that she was gay. Now she says, "I think that I've come to accept myself for who I am, and part of accepting myself is accepting that I'm gay."

While Wendy's experience is well captured by the developmental models, how would stage theorists understand Joan Borman's account of her identity, described in the introduction to this book, in which she did not go through a period of uncertainty and in which she actively reframed her very positive sexual histories with men? In 1989, she said, "I don't think I would have come out if I hadn't been a feminist, because it's not as if I spent a lot of time pining over women physically. I mean, it has been an acquired taste, in a sense. The more time I've spent with women, the more attractive I find women, the more interesting they are to me. And it would not have been enough of an impetus, that alone, nine years ago." Joan did not go through an extended period of questioning; nor was coming to see herself as a lesbian a time filled with pain and anxiety.

How would stage theorists interpret Alex Goldman's account of her sexual identity, which she characterizes as one of "sexual fluidity"? While her attractions to men and to women shift in relation to specific persons, she sees herself as having a "lesbian consciousness," which she continues to maintain even when involved with men, as she was in 1989. Five years later, at the time of the second interview, Alex was in a relationship with a woman. At that point she thought that the term "bisexual lesbian" would fit her situation. Stage theories of sexual identity would characterize Alex as immature, or perhaps as having an "unintegrated personality."

Having passed through the stages of lesbian identity development in her twenties and early thirties, Alex changed her identity in response to changing attractions. Rather than suppress her attractions to men, she chose to act on them and integrate them into her conception of herself.

Stage models of sexual identity development simply do not reflect the experiences of bisexual women like Alex. In addition, stage theorists typically see lesbians' and gay men's identities as essentially synonymous, parallel. And although this would accord with some women's accounts of their sexual identity, like Wendy, it does not articulate the experiences of women such as Joan, who came to a lesbian identity through feminism.

Several critics (Weinberg 1984; Kitzinger 1987) have shrewdly pointed out that stage models of identity development typically reflect the researcher's values, goals, and understandings rather than the research participants'—a problem, no doubt, in other models of identity as well. As social psychologist Celia Kitzinger argues, at the "highest" developmental level, the individual lesbian "believes herself to be essentially the same as heterosexuals, sees her lesbianism as a normal aspect of her 'whole self,' and is integrated into society, trusting and feeling comfortable within the heterosexual world" (1987, p. 54). Kitzinger notes that this conception of lesbian identity reinforces the need for individual psychotherapy, not because lesbians are essentially "sick" but in order to facilitate their "adjustment" and "integration" (see Kitzinger and Perkins 1993 for an expansion of this thesis). In the developmental paradigm, then, adherence to radical lesbian feminism, which views lesbianism as a political identity, or continued immersion in gay and lesbian activism reflects almost a lack of personality integration. That is, lesbian and gay social movement activity, over the long run, might actually *impede* personal growth and maturity by delaying full integration into a heterosexual setting.

Sociological Conceptions of Identity

A second major stream of theorizing about lesbian and gay identity grew out of labeling theory and sociological theories about the self. Drawing on Kinsey's research in the late 1940s and 1950s, Mary McIntosh was one of the first social scientists to use a labeling perspective to challenge the notion that sexual identity is a core, static attribute of personality. In 1968, she wrote, "Many scientists and ordinary people assume that there are two kinds of people in the world: homosexuals and heterosexuals. Some of them recognize that homosexual feelings and behavior are not confined to the persons they would like to call 'homosexuals' and that some of these persons do not actually engage in homosexual behavior." And she noted, "This should pose a crucial problem" (1968, reprinted 1981, p. 30).

McIntosh argued that this conceptualization of homosexuality caused scholars to focus on the wrong questions: on diagnosis of whether an individual was "truly" homosexual or not, and on questions of etiology, or the causes of homosexuality—with an eye toward curing it. Instead, social scientists would be well advised to look at the processes by which individuals become labeled homosexual. Drawing on work in other stigmatized social identities, labeling theorists argued that as individuals are labeled with a stigmatized identity, it becomes more and more difficult for them to choose alternative nondeviant "careers" (see also Plummer 1981). Through a process of socialization, lesbians and gays incorporate ideas about what it means to be lesbian or gay into their own identities. The labeling of an individual's acts as homosexual—both by other lesbians and gays and by the straight world—and the stigmatization of that identity, over time, lead to adoption of a homosexual identity. According to labeling theory (and unlike some earlier psychoanalytic views), homosexual identity per se is not deviant or an indication of psychopathology; however, because it is seen as such by society, a homosexual identity is stigmatized, and individuals with such "spoiled" identities will need to "manage" their interactions in the larger, heterosexual world (Goffman 1963).

In its strictest form, labeling theory has fallen out of favor because of its characterization of homosexuality as "deviant," albeit a socially constructed form of deviance, and its overall lack of support by empirical research (Bell, Weinberg, and Hammersmith 1981). Simply put, it does not appear that individuals become lesbian or gay simply by a process of labeling by others. But the theorists' insight that the labels "homosexual" and "heterosexual" were socially constructed categories proved extremely powerful, and many others took up the banner of constructionism to examine the historical and situational aspects of sexuality.

Social Constructionism

Although social constructionism encompasses a large number of arguments and approaches, these perspectives share the belief that sexualities are constructed in varying ways in different historical contexts and periods, and that lesbian and gay identity as we know it in Western capitalist societies today is historically and culturally specific, dating back at least to the nineteenth century (or, depending on the scholar, earlier; McIntosh, for example, dates it to the turn of the eighteenth century) (Faderman 1991, 1981; D'Emilio 1983; Weeks 1987, 1981). According to constructionists, although homosexual *acts* have been observed in all manner of times and places (and may be near universal), homosexual *actors,* whose identities and lifestyles are organized around their erotic desires for persons of the same gender, are historically specific. In a more radical version of constructionism, others would argue that there are "really" no lesbians and gay men; that is, the categories themselves are evanescent, changing, and arbitrary, and do not refer to "real" categories of persons.

As Edward Stein (1992, p. 6) has noted, philosopher Michel Foucault's *History of Sexuality* (1976) became the *"locus classicus"* of the constructionist program. Foucault traced the development of the homosexual person—as distinct from the earlier sodomite—to the Victorian impulse to categorize sexualities and to create "new specification[s] of individuals" from those categorized (1976, p. 43). In earlier times, a man who had sexual relations with other men may well have been married to a woman and father to multiple children (D'Emilio and Freedman 1988). If caught, he may have been convicted of sodomy, but he would not have been considered a homosexual, one whose nature fundamentally predisposed him toward relationships with others of the same gender. Foucault explained: "As defined by the ancient civil or canonical codes, sodomy was a category of forbidden acts; their perpetrator was nothing more than the juridical subject of them. The nineteenth-century homosexual became a personage, a past, a case history, and a childhood, in addition to being a type of life, a life form, and a morphology, with an indiscreet anatomy and possibly a mysterious physiology. . . . The sodomite had been a temporary aberration; the homosexual was now a species" (1976, p. 43). Discursive practices performed a dual function: both creating the categories and serving as a source of social control over those categorized.

Jeffrey Weeks (1987, 1981), another important constructionist, stressed the role of the sexologists who created a seemingly infinite array of sexual categories from diverse sexual practices. Toward the end of the nineteenth century and the early decades of the twentieth, sexologists such as Havelock Ellis, Richard von Krafft-Ebing, Magnus Hirschfeld, and others worked to create a taxonomy of the various "sexual pathologies." By cataloging and describing the "perverse" and "abnormal," they circumscribed what was "normal" and transformed concerns about the changing relations of men and women in the late nineteenth century into scientific and medical categories. What was normal, according to the sexologists, was a sharp differentiation between the roles and appearances of men and women. A properly "masculine" man and a "feminine" woman naturally formed a heterosexual love object choice. As Weeks thus noted, sexology "is not simply descriptive. It is at times profoundly prescriptive, telling us what we ought to be like, what makes us truly ourselves and 'normal'" (p. 36).

Postmodernism and Queer Theory

Queer theorists add a major voice to the constructionist chorus. Embedded in postmodern and poststructural theories, queer theory attempts to disrupt the fixed categories "homosexual" and "heterosexual." To speak about sexual identity—lesbian identity, or gay identity—implies a unity that betrays the very real differences (of race, class, style, sexual practices) embodied by individuals in diverse social locations and in different moments. Instead of viewing identity as something one *is,* queer theorists, like Diana Fuss (1991), argue for an understanding of identity as difference. In this way, queer theorists point attention to the binary nature of identification. According to Fuss, homosexuality is always implicated in heterosexuality (and vice versa) in a kind of convoluted knot. Creating the "out" lesbian or gay man always brings with it the specter of the closet and its opposite, the heterosexual. The queer theoretical project, thus, is to bring "the hetero/homo opposition to the point of collapse" (1991, p. 1). As Steven Seidman notes, "We are urged to shift our focus from the politics of personal identity to the politics of signification, in particular, to the deconstruction of a hetero/homo code that structures the 'social text' of daily life" (1993, p. 130).

Using the catch-all term "queer" to signify a variety of transgressions, queer theorists seek to challenge the heterosexist status quo. As Michael Warner points out, "Every person who comes to a queer self-understanding knows in one way or another that her stigmatization is connected with gender, the family, notions of individual freedom, the state, public speech, consumption and desire, nature and culture, maturation, reproductive politics, racial and national fantasy, class identity, truth and trust, censorship, intimate life and social display, terror and violence, health care, and deep cultural norms about the bearing of the body. Being queer means fighting about these issues all the time" (1993, p. xiii). At the same time, queer theorists seek to move *beyond* identity itself. Seeing the narrowness and boundary-making inherent in creating categories, queer theorists do not seek to replace more static identities with "better" ones, but instead challenge the boundaries themselves.

There's an exuberant playfulness in much queer writing. But as Steven Seidman notes, there's also an "inching toward textual idealism," a privileging of images and texts, and a refusal to acknowledge the very real social structures and physical bodies—however "dis-organ-ized" (Griggers 1993, p. 179)—in which individuals live. In their emphasis on cultural criticism and their framing of actual social practices as merely discursive, queer theories often remain abstract and typically lack grounding in ordinary women's lives. Further, as a call to action, queer theory can seem politically paralyzing. The critique of identity seems to remain a deconstructive project, not a constructive one, without a vision for a future. As Ken Plummer (1992) points out in his critique of the postmodernist project, "Since there is no grand goal and no chance of progress, what's the point of struggling?" (p. 15). What queer theory misses, in its attempt to take apart the sexual categories, is the role that identities play in ordinary individuals' own lives. Although some are content to remain without labels or embrace the catchall category "queer," others are not. For the latter, the impulse to name the self provides an affirmation—however circumscribed by the imperatives of identity—as well as an impetus to social change.

The Social Constructionist/Essentialist Debates

Paralleling the conflicts around postmodernism and queer theory are a series of acrimonious debates about the "essential" or "constructed" nature of sexual identity. These controversies dominated the discussion of sexual identity through the 1980s (see E. Stein 1992 for an overview). Social constructionists argue that sexual identity is historically and culturally variant. In contrast to those who see homosexuality as something rigid, essentially the same across different cultures and time periods, constructionists believe that lesbian and gay sexual identities arise within specific historical times and places. Although the debate has not been settled, it has generated a great deal of heat, albeit shedding somewhat less light on the nature of sexual identification.

Essentialists argue that something like the modern homosexual and heterosexual have existed in other times and places, and that it is reasonable to posit an unbroken line between earlier homosexuals (such as existed in classical Greece, for example) and today's lesbians and gay men. In all societies, they might argue, there have been homosexuals and heterosexuals (and, perhaps, bisexuals). Some who argue for the essentialist project claim a biological basis for homosexuality (e.g., Bell, Weinberg, and Hammersmith 1981; see also the articles in parts 2 and 3 of McWhirter, Sanders, and Reinisch 1990). Yet, as historian John Boswell (1992) has noted, few scholars actually embrace the label "essentialist," and in fact most scholars (at least the historians) who have been so labeled by others do incorporate tenets of social constructionism in their work.

Others have also suggested that the differences between the two points of view are more apparent than real. James Weinrich (1992), for example, argues that *both* essentialist and constructionist points of view are correct. Various societies clearly interpret sexual acts between members of the same sex in different ways. The *berdache* tradition of some Native American tribes in which men and sometimes women took on the social and sexual roles of the other gender included a spiritual dimension. In this context, the socially sanctioned intimate relations of the *berdache* are clearly unlike those of modern U.S. lesbians and gay men. On the other hand, Weinrich argues, there are some cross-cultural continuities, including what he calls "gender inversion," "role playing," and "age-biased" homosexuality.

The debates about whether or not lesbian or gay identity is socially constructed, and if lesbians and gays can be said to constitute a "real" group, sometimes become polarized around the question of choice: whether lesbians and gay men *choose* to be gay. Some argue that choice is a function of gender: Men are less likely to say that they chose a gay identity, and women more so. Rarely do accounts of bisexual identity figure into this picture. While it is important to examine narratives of choice, it is also important to understand how sexual identities may be imposed from outside the individual. People do not select freely from a menu of identities; rather, cultural ideals and social institutions shape the identities that may be chosen. For those who experience same-sex desire in the United States today, it is difficult to resist a lesbian, gay, or bisexual identity.

Ultimately, as Steven Epstein argues in a carefully crafted essay, neither constructionism nor essentialism provides a complete explanation of human sexuality (1987). In its most extreme form, social constructionism would predict an endlessly multiplying array of sexualities across cultures and time periods; essentialism, in its most extreme form, would predict only two or—at most—three sexual categories. The historical reality is somewhere between the two. While sexualities are clearly malleable and fluid, they are fluid only within certain ranges. Societies do not organize sexuality completely arbitrarily.

At the same time, neither side offers complete insight into the beliefs and political practices of lesbian, gay, and bisexual people.

Neither constructionism nor essentialism completely accounts for the complexities of individuals' understandings of their sexuality. As Steven Epstein has pointed out, while academics and intellectuals are busying themselves with deconstructing the categories, lesbian and gay activists (and, increasingly, bisexuals as well) are, ironically, loudly proclaiming their identities—and in the process making rigid and fixed the categories themselves (1987). To many living in lesbian and gay communities, their identities feel solid and fixed—an essential and unchanging part of who they "really" are— and a number of lesbian and gay organizations have crafted political strategies based on that notion. As Wendy Hammond describes it, "None [of my identities] is as important as being gay . . . If someone said, 'You have to give up your job to be gay,' I would be fine. I mean, how could I live otherwise?" For women like Wendy, there is nothing arbitrary or chosen about her sexuality—it is simply what she *is*.

On the other hand, some lesbian feminists have argued for a political construction of lesbianism (see, e.g., Rich 1980; Kitzinger 1987; Hoagland and Penelope 1988; Radicalesbians 1970). In the heyday of radical lesbian feminism, some argued that *any* woman could be a lesbian. If relationships with men are oppressive, then one route to political and social transformation is to separate from men and form relationships with women. While a political construction of lesbianism is perhaps less common, especially in the 1980s and 1990s, many women do in fact feel some element of choice in living a lesbian or bisexual life. Chrissy Herek, a young white woman just coming into a bisexual identity, did not think that her sexuality was political. But she did feel that bisexuality is "a choice for all . . . that is potentially in almost every woman to make. But that a big percentage, just because of society, won't accept an open door."

Other constructions of lesbian/gay sexuality also flourish. In recent attempts to pass legislation that would prohibit the inclusion of lesbians, gay men, and bisexuals in civil rights statutes, the religious right has reverted to earlier, sin-based notions of homosexuality. Claiming that homosexuality is chosen—and immoral—behavior, they have argued that lesbians and gays do not form a distinct group and should therefore not be protected against discrimination in housing and employment. Some gays and lesbians have responded by attempting to document a biological basis for homosexuality; if homosexual behavior and identity are not chosen, they argue, then homosexuals should not be discriminated against. Others argue for the existence of a sexual *orientation,* apart from whatever sexual practices and identities individuals may hold. For them, sexual orientation—the feelings of sexual attraction to others of the same sex—may be biologically based; but sexual identities—the cognitive labeling of oneself as a gay man or a lesbian—are shaped in whatever ways specific cultures and societies fashion for those with same-sex attractions. Still others argue that however sexual orientation or identity is formed, lesbians and gays constitute a bona fide minority group—at least in late twentieth century United States. As such, civil rights protections are needed to protect against attacks on civil liberties such as those posed by the religious right.

As these recent debates have amply demonstrated, questions of sexual identity are inherently political. In the larger scheme, it may not really matter if sexual identities are constructed or essential, whether today's gay men are "really" like ancient Athenians, or whether 1970s radical dykes are "really" similar to the passionate friendships of nineteenth century upper-class white women. What *is* clear is that in the late twentieth century, sexuality is contested terrain and while sexual identities may serve as a source of social control and normalization (as the postmodernists rightly claim), they also engender feelings of pride and resistance to what Dorothy Smith calls the "relations of ruling" (1987).

As Steven Epstein argues, the debates between constructionism and essentialism are, in part, debates about choice *and* constraint.

And once we abandon the extremes of both positions, "we can recognize that a gay or lesbian identity might have a clear resonance for individuals without necessarily binding them to any specific definition of what that identity 'means.' An intermediate position allows us to recognize that these sexual identities are *both inescapable and transformable,* and are capable of giving rise to a variety of political expressions" (1987, reprinted 1992, pp. 273–74; emphasis in original).

Epstein's comments are useful in helping to orient us toward the very real needs, beliefs, and priorities of ordinary lesbians, bisexuals, and gay men. In the end, the underlying nature of sexual identity—whether an underlying sexual orientation exists, whether identities are simply made up, or whether there is no underlying identity at all—is not the most important question. Although these questions may have their uses, the debates have become sterile. Far more important are the real and varied accounts women tell about who they are and how they came to be that way—and the implications of these accounts for building social networks and political alliances. Whatever the usefulness of queer theory in pointing out the boundaries and rigidities of identification—and these are not minimal—as long as queer theory remains at the level of texts, it cannot help us understand the very real concerns of ordinary lesbians and bisexual women, most of whom have never heard of a floating signifier, let alone considered it had anything to do with their sexuality.

At the same time, queer theory and social constructionism point to the need to focus on the multiplicity of identities and accounts of change and fluidity in women's life stories. Individuals clearly experience themselves as complex and multifaceted, with race and ethnic identities, occupational identities, and family identities to name just a few. Although sexual identities are among the most salient (and contested) in our contemporary society, so are race, ethnicity, and gender. We need to see how lesbian, gay, and bisexual identities are acted out in the context of overlapping allegiances. For lesbians, being a woman—in whatever idiosyncratic or socially patterned way—may be just as important as, and inseparable from, being a lesbian. For lesbians of color, race and ethnicity may not be disconnected from their gender and sexuality. As Audre Lorde wrote in 1984, "As a Black lesbian feminist comfortable with the many different ingredients of my identity, and a woman committed to racial and sexual freedom from oppression, I find I am constantly being encouraged to pluck out one aspect of myself and present this as a meaningful whole, eclipsing or denying the other parts of self. But this is a destructive and fragmenting way to live" (p. 120). Theories of identity must clearly take this multiplicity into account.

Theories of identity must also capture the variability—and the contingency—of women's sexual identities. Women create their senses of who they are within particular relationships and within particular social and political contexts. Women who came out prior to the gay liberation movement, such as Kate Foster, faced a very different set of choices and options than women who came out at the height of lesbian feminism, like Sally Zimmerman and Joan Borman. Women who in the 1990s see a visible bisexual presence within the lesbian and gay movement may interpret attractions to both men and women very differently from those who experienced the same desires in the 1950s. Whatever theories of identity ultimately persist, it is clear that the broad spectrum of theories filters into individual women's own accounts of their identities. What is striking is that individuals' identity accounts are far more varied than even the constructionist literature would lead one to believe.

2

Cover Stories

> The story of identity is a cover story. A cover story for
> making you think you stayed in the same place, al-
> though with another bit of your mind you do know that
> you've moved on. What we've learned about the struc-
> ture of the way in which we identify suggests that iden-
> tification is not one thing, one moment. We have now
> to reconceptualize identity as a process of identification,
> and that is a different matter. It is something that hap-
> pens over time, that is never absolutely stable, that is
> subject to the play of history and the play of difference.
>
> STUART HALL (1989, p. 15)

Susan Becker, a native Southerner, has been calling herself a lesbian since 1976, the year she became involved with a woman.
In the area of the deep South she is from: "I was never taught that
homosexuality was *bad,* particularly, it just was a world that didn't
exist. Because we didn't know anything about it, it never occurred
to me that I might be a lesbian until I met this woman, fell in love,
and thought, 'Oh! That's why I didn't like kissin' the guys!'"

Now in her early forties and working in a high-level professional job at the university, she says, being a lesbian "means that I
choose to make love with women and have physical relationships
with women. And my primary world is made up of women—very
few men." Although at an earlier time in her life Susan was very
closeted, she is now proud to be lesbian, a stance she sees as having political connotations. That "may be the reason why a lot of
my friends, who are also lesbians, don't use the word *lesbian.* Because they think it means totally exclusive of men or rejecting
them, which *I* don't think it means."

Defining Lesbianism

To outsiders, defining lesbianism is simple—or relatively so. According to most dictionary definitions, a lesbian is a "female homosexual," a woman who has sexual desire for or relations with women. Ultimately, in outsiders' accounts, lesbianism boils down to sex. Although to some lesbians, like Wendy Hammond and Bonita Brown, sexuality is what lesbianism is primarily about, to others, lesbian identity can take on a variety of different meanings, which may or may not include sexual relationships with women.

The women interviewed and surveyed referred to at least four different dimensions of lesbian identity. In defining for themselves what it means to be a lesbian, they included (1) having sexual relations with women, (2) having emotional relationships with women, (3) making their friendships and social relationships with women central to their lives, and (4) seeing their relationships with women as having a political dimension. Some felt that the *person,* not the gender, was important in defining their relationships. The women varied in terms of which of these were most important. While maintaining sexual relationships with women—or desiring them— might seem to be the lowest common denominator in all the definitions, not all agreed that a woman must be or have been or even prefer to be sexual with women to be called a lesbian.

LOVERS AND FRIENDS: For Sarah Greene, a Quaker who lives in a rural area outside of town and makes friends with great difficulty, being a lesbian "means that I choose to have my primary relationships with women, and choose to put [the] time and energy that I spend relating to people into being with other women." Likewise, Marcela Reyes says, "I'm a woman who loves other women and prefers to have relationships with women."

Some women's lesbian identity is defined primarily by the importance of social and romantic relationships with women. Unlike others who may stress the political or sexual dimensions of lesbianism, these women emphasize the friendships and love relationships they have developed with women. In the survey, they agree strongly that their "most satisfying social relationships are with other women." They emphasize their feelings of love for women, claiming to "feel most comfortable when around other lesbians." Women who expressed this identity account felt that they've "always had close relationships with women and girls." These women are clear that, for them, lesbianism is *not* strictly a sexual identity. They disagree strongly with the statement, "Being a lesbian means simply being sexually attracted to other women."

Even though she now sees it as outdated and "quaint," Ilene Zemke, a writer in her late thirties, feels that the term "woman-identified woman" more closely fits her identity. When interviewed in 1989, she said, "Most of my friends and people I have closest contacts with are women, although not exclusively lesbian. . . . My world centers around women, and that makes me feel that I live in a lesbian world. . . . Lowest on the scale of what it is that makes me a lesbian is sexuality. I put that at the very bottom."

Susan Becker emphasized the joys of connecting with women: "There's nothing I don't like [about being a lesbian]. The things that I find particularly positive about it are knowing other lesbians, being able to relate in a variety of other ways . . . I like the variety of women that I talk to. I like knowing other women."

Social and emotional bonding with women is by far the most important aspect of these women's identities. For them, it is important to be relatively private about their sexual orientation. Although they believe—to a limited extent—that it is important to be out, they are less likely to confront others openly. They agree with the statement: "I don't usually tell people about my sexual orientation, but I don't hide it either. I just live my life and let people figure it out." They also tend to feel that it's not "anyone's business what people do with their sexuality." Deena King echoed this sentiment. "I don't have to tell people," she said. "They usually figure it out, and the subject never comes up."

While these women tend to call themselves feminists, they do not experience their lesbianism as a political—or as a personal—choice. They are less likely than others to see their lesbianism and their feminism as connected, and they disagree that lesbianism is a choice, especially for themselves. Instead, they are more likely to feel that they were born lesbian. As Deena King related, she thinks homosexuality is genetic. Similarly, Susan Becker felt that women cannot choose.

Overall, these women do not see themselves as bisexual; nor do they find relationships with men particularly attractive. After her first long-term love relationship with a woman ended, Susan Becker attempted a relationship with a man. It became quickly apparent that heterosexuality was not for her. "It wasn't that he was a particularly awful lover, it was just that it seemed very unnatural to me. Heterosexual sex seemed very unnatural, and it seemed very violent. And violent to me in a very primitive way of pure physical need as opposed to making love for pleasure and emotion as well as physical sensation."

POLITICS: Others, like Kate Foster, include a political dimension to their self-definitions. For Kate, being a lesbian means not being subordinate to a man, being her own social actor. "I feel that being a lesbian, in spite of the restrictions, means that people simply don't expect me to be like everybody else, like every other female. . . . Even my incredibly sexist brother-in-law will talk about me as being my own person. I could not have been that had I not been a lesbian." Similarly, Katharine Williams, a white woman in her forties who has been very active in lesbian and gay politics, sees it as a statement that she's not living up to the mainstream's idea of what a woman should be. She actively resists media images that depict women in stereotyped ways. Although sexuality is included in both Kate and Katharine's accounts of their sexual identities, disrupting gender patterns and asserting an autonomous female presence are an important part of what it means for them to be lesbian.

This politicized identity account has its roots in the lesbian/gay movement, as well as in feminist ideology, which sees relationships with men as rooted in inequality. In keeping with the feminist slogan "the personal is political" and the blatant, "in-your-face" politics of queer activist groups, this account suggests that coming out as a lesbian disrupts heterosexist assumptions about lesbians and increases lesbian visibility. This position is also consistent with the arguments about coming out set forth by many gay and lesbian activists, ranging from the more conservative Marshall Kirk and Hunter Madsen (1989), who wish to show that lesbians and gay men are "just like" heterosexuals, to the more flamboyant tactics of Act Up and Queer Nation, who emphasize queer visibility. If all gays and lesbians were open about their sexual orientation, the argument maintains, increased public acceptance would have to follow because heterosexuals would realize simply how many lesbians and gay men there are (D'Emilio 1983).

Being lesbian or bisexual is an important part of these women's identities—perhaps one of the most important aspects. And they very much define themselves by their sexuality. Women who embrace this identity account care deeply that lesbians make a visible presence in the world. Whether they take a more radical activist stance or a more quiet political strategy, they strongly agree that "it's important to be out about my sexual orientation as much as possible."

Leslie Mohr and Patrice Amaro both discussed the political implications of being out. Leslie talks about coming out in terms of obligation: "I have to come out all the time because people don't look at me and say, 'She must be a lesbian.'" Similarly, Patrice feels that it is important to make a lesbian presence known, especially at work, and especially when the topic of oppression comes up, as it often does in her job. "Then I feel it's very important to say something; and I usually will preface it by saying, 'Well, as a lesbian, this is how I feel about it . . .' Because I feel it's important for people to know there's another person present, and that especially when there are people of color in the room, that the realization is that there are other people here, too, that are—I don't like the word minority—but oppressed. And rather than just having this homophobia word thrown around with no one there, or noticeable to them. So in that way I'm out."

This identity account emphasizes the connections between feminism and lesbianism. These women proudly call themselves feminists, and for at least some, feminism may have influenced their decisions to come out. Deb Smith has been both a feminist and a lesbian for over twenty years. As she thinks back, she says, "The more I really got into feminism, then the more comfortable I was calling myself a lesbian." Similarly, Patrice Amaro "definitely" sees the two as connected. To be a feminist helps her "to be proud of who [she is]." Although she knows that some lesbians are not feminists, she says, "In my case, the two are very much a part of each other."

At least some of the women who endorsed this account were not sure if they would have come out were it not for their feminism. And they tended to have identified as feminists prior to coming out as lesbians. At least in small part, they see their lesbianism as a choice. Joan Borman echoes this response. "If I view it as a sexual reality," she argues, "then what's absolutely real to me is that I chose to be a lesbian." Joan was adamant about the ordering of her lesbianism and her feminism: "I don't think I would have come out if I hadn't been a feminist."

Leslie Mohr was also clear that her sexual identity and her feminism are related. "I feel like I would never assume that lesbians are always feminists, but I can't imagine being a lesbian unless I was a feminist. . . . And in fact, I know that one of the reasons that it's not attractive for me to be involved with a man is because I feel as if the struggle against sexism is so important in my life that I want my lover to be an ally in that struggle on the same side that I'm on." As she sees it, her feminism is linked not only to her lesbian identity but also to her awareness of the oppression of others. "I feel as if I came out in the context of the women's movement. I also feel as if my politics came from the women's movement and . . . my awareness of race and class issues and of homophobia and the necessity of resisting all those forms of oppression. I would not have become interested in those issues if I hadn't become interested in the oppression of women and in sexism as a structure."

While these women may have experienced their sexuality as a choice, they emphatically do not see themselves as bisexual. I asked Joan Borman in 1994 why, given her marriage and her early history of positive relationships with men, she did not think of herself as bisexual. For Joan, bisexuality was a decidedly unattractive proposition: "It just does not make any sense to me." Even if they decided to have sex with a man, these women would probably continue to see themselves as lesbian.

At the same time—and like the first identity account—this account stresses the importance of intimate and social relationships with girls and women. The emphasis on the political meanings of lesbianism is combined with a deep and abiding love for and friendship with women. For the most part, these women feel most comfortable when around other lesbians. As Joan Borman describes it, "I live in a world where my assumption is that the kind of emotional, affectionate, physical, sexual, and intellectual rapport is going to be with other women. And for the most part I find lesbians easier to be with than straight women."

Many of the women in this group are active in the Gay, Lesbian, and Bisexual Task Force and other political institutions: women's studies, the battered women's shelter, and so forth. In emphasizing the importance of being public about lesbian identity, this account expresses an activist point of view that sees openness about lesbianism as an important way to make social and political change. When I returned to the city in 1994, I heard about several attempts to make lesbian lives visible during a struggle for increased civil rights protection. In one demonstration, I was told about a group of women who brought their books and rocking chairs downtown and simply sat, rocking and reading, near a placard that read, "Lesbians reading." It is this type of activism that accords with this identity account.

"IT'S THE PERSON, NOT THE GENDER": "Before I was involved with G., I think I felt that I could have gotten involved with either a man or a woman," Alex Goldman said. "It had to do with the person that came along." When she first became involved with a woman, she remembered that "one of the things I said early on . . . was that my getting involved had nothing to do with men. I didn't hate men."

A third identity account entails an openness toward bisexuality and a more positive attitude toward relationships with men than is expressed by the other two accounts. Women who endorse this identity account have had significant love relationships with men, and they are more likely to experience their underlying sexual orientation as bisexual. Cheryl Cook clearly expresses this position: "I have never *not* felt that I was bisexual," she claimed.

These women feel vehemently that being a lesbian does not entail rejecting men, and they are open to relationships with men in the future. Laurel Jameson says, "I'm definitely lesbian-identified, yet I also include men in my life." Unlike others, they do not interpret their past relationships with men as inconsistent with their current identities. Instead, they tend to rate their past relationships with men fairly positively. In 1989, when Alex Goldman talked about her sexual attractions, she said, "At the level of gut response, I'm probably more attracted to men than to women," a sentiment echoed by Jan Liebow, a bisexual woman in her thirties. But even when involved with a man, she still maintained a strong sense of lesbian consciousness, and she was still attracted to women.

For women who endorse this account, qualities of the individual person may be more important than gender in forming relationships. Chrissy Herek described this position: "If there's a man who coincides with my needs and what I look for in a person, and if he's male, he's male. If it's the qualities I look for, then that's who I'll be with."

Yet relationships with women are clearly very important to these women. They rated their loves and friendships with women as among their most satisfying, and they tended to feel that they had always had close relationships with women and girls. Again, Chrissy Herek expressed this position: "I just receive more from women. And I'm more comforted and more happy. . . . Women just treat me with much more respect and love and affection."

As with the other identity accounts, privacy issues are important. Although bisexual women have increasingly been organizing autonomously, not all bisexual women have a separate community available to them (see Queen 1992; Hutchins and Kaahumanu 1991; Weise 1992). In this town, a bisexual community was only just beginning to form in the late 1980s; by the early 1990s, it seemed little stronger. Because of this lack of community, being open about their sexual identity may be especially risky for bisexual women or for lesbians who acknowledge having significant relationships with men. While heterosexuals may not accept bisexual women because of their relationships with women, lesbians may not fully accept them because of their relationships with men. In fact, some have argued that lesbians are even more hostile to bisexual women than heterosexuals are (Rust 1992a). Women who endorse this account tend neither to tell people about their sexual orientation nor to hide it. And they prefer not to define themselves by their sexuality.

Cheryl Cook is, in general, very private about revealing information about her sexuality, a stance that has been consistent over the years. "I don't talk about it at all. . . . Number one, I don't wear my heart on my sleeve. Number two, you know, my personal life is my personal life, and I don't talk about it with a lot of people." Although she sees her reticence as deeply rooted in her personality and in her need to maintain an active business and professional life, it still serves to protect her from some of the criticism of both the lesbian and heterosexual communities.

Yet the women who subscribe to this identity account are clearly not apolitical. Feminism is very important to them, and may, at least for some, be connected with their sexual identity. To a greater extent than the other identity accounts, this account stresses sexual identity as a matter of choice, not as a matter of birth or predestination. Somewhat paradoxically, however, these women do not see lesbianism as a *political* choice. In keeping with their emphasis on privacy, lesbian or bisexual identity may be an individual or a personal choice, rather than a political choice.

In sum, this final identity account centers around bisexuality and the importance of relationships with men. Although not all who endorsed this account thought of themselves as bisexual, all acknowledged that they had had significant relationships with men and might consider a relationship with a man in the future. For them, the *person,* not the gender, was most important in defining their attractions. At the same time, the account also stresses the importance of social and romantic relationships with women, the desire for privacy around disclosing their sexual identity, and, to a lesser extent, the possibilities of choice in coming to a lesbian or bisexual identity.

Coming-Out Narratives: Interpreting the Self

Taking on a lesbian or bisexual identity involves a process of interpreting one's emotions and experiences and seeing them as relevant to sexual identity. Out of all their memories, women picked *these* events and emotions, and not others, as having relevance for their sexual identities. Coming-out stories, perhaps one of the most prolific forms of lesbian writing, tell women how to interpret and recast their own past experiences to bring them in line with their current identities (see, e.g., Stanley and Wolfe 1980; Baetz 1980; Lewis 1979). From my own period of "coming out" in the late 1970s and early 1980s, for example, I recall hearing stories of crushes on camp counselors and gym teachers and adolescent sex play with other girls. If lesbians were mannish women, or women who had crushes on gym teachers, how could I be a lesbian? I had never been to summer camp, wasn't especially fond of gym, and had never kissed another girl. I found myself frantically searching through my memories, trying to find evidence that my past experiences were consistent with my newly forming lesbian identity.

FALLING IN LOVE: When Penny Peck fell in love with a woman for the second time, in the middle of the 1960s, she fell hard. Time seemed to stop when she and her lover looked into each other's eyes: "We spent a lot of quiet hours just holding each other. Nothing else. One would make a statement. It might take one or two hours for the other to respond, to make sure that the words were exactly right. And then another long stretch of time would go by. Do a response to that one. We spent just hours doing that. There wasn't any chit-chatting in between. Just a very deep searching to make sure that all the words that came out of our mouths were right."

In the mid-1970s, Wendy Hammond fell in love. She said, "I really felt the purest love I ever felt in my life . . . and I walked into it like a child." Although the relationship eventually turned out to be a "disaster," Wendy said, "I believed, when I got into that relationship, that you meet somebody, and that you fall in love, and that you live happily every after. I probably would have written it down and sworn to it."

The experience of falling in love or becoming sexually involved with a woman made many women consider whether they might be lesbian or bisexual. Although some time may have elapsed between the initial feelings of attraction and self-identification as lesbian or bisexual—for one woman, it took over twenty years—nearly all of the women, at least in retrospect, saw these feelings as relevant to their current sexual identity.

Falling in love was not the only clue that one might be lesbian. Other commonly mentioned themes included having crushes on girls or women, failing to be attracted to boys and men, and firsthand contact with other lesbians or bisexuals. The latter category—personal contact—seems particularly important for women who did *not* recall having crushes on other girls and women. Accounts of gender nonconformity—being a tomboy, rebelling against traditional girl's roles—also figure prominently in women's stories of how they came to see themselves as lesbian or bisexual.

Ilene Zemke came to feel that she was a lesbian based, literally, on a dream that she had when she was in her early twenties. She recounted in 1989, "I had a male lover. We had been together for two years. One night we were sleeping together, and I dreamed that I was sleeping next to a woman. And it felt very good. In the dream it was very warm, and it . . . just felt absolutely right. And I reached out my hand, because in the dream the presence of another person was so close and real. So I reached out my hand, and in fact there was another person there, and I remember feeling that person's body and skin. And my hand went up to his face, and he had a very full beard. And I felt his beard, and it was very scratchy and it woke me up. And I woke up and saw—of course here I was next to my lover—and thought, 'Oh, no. It's a man.' . . . The feeling of being next to a woman, and the acute disappointment I felt when it was a man stuck in my mind." After a second, similar dream, "There would be no doubt that I would not have relations with men any more." Following a period of time in which she was celibate, Irene came to identify herself as a radical feminist and moved closer and closer to seeing herself as a lesbian.

Krista Larrson, a young white woman interviewed in 1989, also came to see herself as a lesbian in response to a series of dreams. As a first-year student at college, she found herself with a "big crush" on a woman, and she remembered thinking "maybe I'm a lesbian. And I decided no, I wasn't a lesbian . . . because I still felt I was in love with a man that I knew and was still interested in thinking about being involved with men." It wasn't until later, when she began to have erotic dreams about women, that she began to see herself as a lesbian. "I think my desire to be with women got a lot stronger. And I think it actually was dreams. When I started actually having sexual dreams about women, that made it hit home." To make the leap between thinking of herself as a lesbian and living what felt to her like a lesbian life, she left school and began working in a place "where there were a lot of dykes." There, people could just assume she was a lesbian and she wouldn't have to come out and actively tell people.

FEELING DIFFERENT: The feeling of being different is probably one of the most often-mentioned cues to a lesbian or gay identity. While most people, lesbian or not, probably think of themselves as different or unique in one way or another, lesbians and bisexual women are likely to interpret that feeling of difference as evidence of a lesbian or bisexual identity. Sometimes that feeling of difference is expressed as an awareness that one is gender discrepant: liking boys' games and toys instead of girls', being a tomboy. Other times the difference is experienced as a sense of marginality, or being outside other children's or adolescents' social circles.

Alex Goldman theorizes that "girls that don't fit neatly into the kind of idiotic sex role standards, and who feel themselves to be different from a young age—you know, they like trucks, they like guns, they don't like dolls, they like to do rough and tumble play. I was thinking that maybe what happens to those girls is that they define themselves as different from other girls. . . . If they don't identify with all the stupid little things that girls do, they also don't identify with getting married, having babies, so they don't identify with the heterosexuality of it. . . . Their sense of being different just gets expanded into the sexual realm."

Wendy Hammond said she always felt much more comfortable with the boys than with the girls. "I could never picture myself with a man in any kind of relationship other than maybe playing baseball." Growing up in the 1960s, forced to wear dresses, "I always felt in disguise in the world."

Denny Slater, a working-class white woman in her late thirties, also felt different. As a child, she struggled with the trappings of femininity that were forced on her. "There was a lot of force to convince me to accept those dolls and to accept wearing dresses. I thought it was foolish. I thought it was foolish when I was little to have to wear my snowpants, and then take them off, you know. Why can't I just wear pants and have my legs warm? That made absolutely no sense to me, even as a child. I struggled with that, and I fought with that; and I didn't like my hair being put in curlers or spoolies or the torture my mother put me in to prove that she had a girl."

Surely many heterosexual women were "tomboys" as well, or felt different because they were fat or wore glasses, didn't like boys as much as they liked books, didn't like the games they had to play to be accepted, or were just plain unpopular. Yet these experiences don't lead heterosexual women to think of themselves as lesbian.

Accounts of gender discrepancy become one of the ways in which lesbians recast their childhood and adolescent histories to construct an unbroken line between their past selves and their current lesbian identities.

THE LURE OF LESBIANISM: Other women felt that contact with other lesbians—both in person and through reading—was important in their coming out. Essentially, other lesbians showed these women the possibilities for living a life with women and gave them a way to name their desires. Leslie Mohr contrasts two periods in her life: before reading about and meeting other lesbians, and after. "When I first started to think that word might apply to me, it makes me remember before I came out, [when] I was twenty, and I had a very intense friendship with a woman that I was living with. And we talked about the possibility that we might want to be lovers. And we were both just getting into feminism, too, and we were talking about how it seemed as if there was something kind of coercive about the way in which we kept having to construct the men around us as their best possible selves in order to find them at all attractive, whereas the women in our lives seemed so much more attractive to us without that kind of extra effort.

"But at the time, I don't remember using the word 'lesbian' at all. . . . And I think that was because I didn't know any lesbians. . . . And I certainly didn't know anything about lesbian community or anything like that. So I didn't think, 'Am I a lesbian?' then. . . . I think I thought, 'Could I have a homosexual relationship with A.?' And I don't think I ever thought that would mean that I was gay, you know. Then, in a kind of homosexual panic, I quickly got involved with a man and stayed with him for a couple of years." Finally, Leslie met a woman to whom she was really attracted. Still, she said, "I really think I'm somebody who came out via text. By that time I had done a lot of reading, and even though

I still didn't know any lesbians, it was a word that was part of my vocabulary, and I could see a relation between feminism and lesbianism that I think I had wanted to deny when I was first getting involved in feminism." Becoming a lesbian "was a possibility that was opened up for me by my reading and by my knowledge that there were lesbians in the world."

In the early 1970s when she was eighteen, and in a very different context, Denny Slater also began to think that she might be a lesbian because of her contact with other lesbians. She said, "the woman who was my best friend turned out to be a lesbian. So I got to witness her relationship. And while I was witnessing her relationship and my feelings toward her and my acceptance of who she was, [I] realized that I wasn't afraid of being close to someone who was homosexual. . . . It didn't interfere with my closeness to her or my intimacy with her. And by sharing with her, I realized that I felt strongly about women. . . . And so I came out when I was twenty. And I was very relieved. I identified immediately with the intimacy."

Choice *and* Constraint?

Whether one can choose to be lesbian or bisexual, or whether that is something one just *is,* is hotly contested, not only among academics but among lesbians and bisexuals themselves. Some argue that people are born lesbian or bisexual, or become so at a very early age. Others argue that sexuality is more malleable, fluid (Golden 1987, 1994; see also Whisman 1996) and, at least for some people, includes a degree of volition. At the height of the feminist movement during the 1970s, some women saw lesbianism as a choice that virtually all women could make. The most influential statements of lesbian feminism redefined lesbianism in terms of women's political and emotional bonding with women (Rich 1980; Radicalesbians 1970). In a male-dominated society, to choose relationships with men was to side with the patriarchy. If lesbians were woman-identified women, then *any* woman could choose to be a lesbian.

While lesbian feminism and its more radical conceptions of choice have never been the predominant political theory held by lesbians, it became influential among some lesbians in the 1970s and early 1980s, especially among young lesbians on college campuses (Whisman 1991, p. 4). Still, many women surely came to a lesbian identity through conscious reflection in the feminist movement. At the very least, the feminist movement brought many women into contact with one another in the course of working together politically. The movement enabled those who sought sexual and emotional relationships with women to find each other.[1]

Notions of choice clearly enter into lesbians' and bisexual women's accounts of their identities. Even if they have not "settled" the question for themselves (probably the most common position), lesbians and bisexual women clearly deliberate that question. Marcela's response was revealing. "I hate this question. I hate this 'cause I've been struggling with this for a long time. Part of me says 'yes' because I could choose to be with a man, but I don't know how long lasting that would be. If that would really be what I wanted, what I would enjoy, what I would want out of my life. . . . Choice. Aargh! Such a hard one. It's hard to say, I guess, because I see so many people come out after they've been in heterosexual relationships for years. And it looks like a choice has been made. But who's to say they were miserable those entire years? . . . Can you choose to be lesbian? I can't say. I don't know for sure."

Marcela's response ("maybe") was probably the most prevalent among the women I spoke with. "Maybe" covers three positions. First, some thought that women can choose to act against what feels natural or right to them. Although these women are most comfortable being with women, they could choose to act contrary to those feelings and be with a man. Others saw the issue on a more global scale: Some women can choose, and others cannot. The third position was an unsettled one: They really didn't know if women could choose to be lesbian or not, or they took a variety of positions that were more or less consistent with each other. A smaller number felt very certainly and strongly that it was not a choice, and a very few felt adamantly that it was.

Anne Biersmith's position was unsettled. One of the few interviewees who still felt a great deal of discomfort with her sexuality, Anne vacillated among a variety of positions. "Here's the whole range of how I think. Sometimes I think yes, I'm a lesbian, I have always been, always will be, and it's inherent and ingrained and all of that. All the way to—there are other things that we're addicted to that we shouldn't be, too, you know? There are other things that we're drawn to, or inclined toward, that we need to look at . . . So that's the whole range, and I'm everywhere and in-between."

Later in the interview, she interpreted choice in another way. "I have a sneaking suspicion that we can choose. . . . Yes, definitely we can choose what to deny in our lives and what to go with. . . . I guess everything is a choice. . . . Let's take this as an example. Everybody in the world is inclined toward having a relationship, right? And for some people, their choice to be celibate, say, goes against how they are, goes against their nature, maybe. And I don't think that life is only about looking at what we like to do best, and then going with that. I think it's much more positive than that."

Still later, Anne said, "Let's get in touch with our source, and let's get in touch with God, and then we won't have to fight with any of this stuff about 'am I lesbian?' [And] what does that mean? I don't think it's cool to decide you're a lesbian, and then go find one. . . . And I don't think that straight people should do that, either. We should be falling in love with *people*. . . . I think there's some lesbians who are cutting off half the population here, and I don't think that's cool. Maybe they shouldn't do that. And so to decide ahead of time is putting God in a box, I think."

Although clearly not coming from a religious background, Denny Slater also takes a variety of positions on choice. Echoing the radical lesbians of the 1970s, she said, "I think that all women are lesbians. I think it has to do with intimacy. In our society, I think to be with a man is to choose abuse. That's negating one's self, because they have power over us in this society. If that did not exist, then I think people would have freedom to choose." When asked specifically if *she* chose to be lesbian, she said, "I feel that I choose to take the responsibilities of the society. Again, I think, given my understanding of my energy, that I've always been a lesbian. I've just been more in touch, I think, with myself."

Like Denny Slater and Anne Biersmith, Patrice Amaro also has contradictory feelings about the issue of choice. When she first talked about identifying as a lesbian, she said, "I don't know what I would be like if, indeed, the society were much more accepting of everyone. So in that sense, I can't say. Because for me it's not, 'Well, I've always been sexually attracted to women,' because—I mean, this may sound really dumb . . . it's sort of like, you know, there's certain liquors or something that you gain a taste for. . . . I can't say that I was necessarily sexually attracted to men or sexually attracted to women, as much as that's how you're raised."

Patrice sees that women can become lesbian in many different ways. "I believe that there are women who choose to be lesbians and are sexually with men. I think because of what the definition of a lesbian means to me—which is a woman-identification—a lot of women I know are very much spiritually, politically attached and bonded to women, but maybe sexually connected with men. . . . They're choosing to be sexually heterosexual, but are lesbian. . . . And there are also women, I think, who choose to be lesbian because they're not finding the support and satisfaction within the patriarchal system." When asked if she specifically chose to be lesbian, she said, "Yes . . . This is going to contradict what I said earlier, but in some ways I feel like I've always been lesbian. So that it's sort of like I've kind of migrated to a place that is accepting for me. I don't know if I really chose it, you know? I didn't sit around and go, 'Oh, today, this is what I'm going to do,' as much as I feel that was home for me, that was my niche."

Perhaps the most common position on choice was articulated by Louise Pratt in 1989. As she wryly noted, "I could have chosen not to be a lesbian, and I probably would have ended up very unhappy. But I mean that's a choice that was open to me." She further reflected, "And even choosing to be a lesbian certainly did not make me happy for a long time. . . . When I look at sexuality my view is that it's really a way of expressing love for another person. And I think that we all choose who we express that love with." In 1994, however, Louise no longer thought of herself as a lesbian. If she can choose to be a lesbian, then she can choose not to be one as well.

In a process reminiscent of labeling theory, Kate Foster felt that at one point she had a choice, but after so many years of living as a lesbian, she couldn't imagine living her life otherwise. "I think that I am comfortable enough with men and also sexually comfortable enough with men that had lesbianism not been presented to me as an alternative I would have been functional. At the same time, I feel that the far greater part of my sexual orientation, even at the time I was in my teens, was toward women." By the time Kate was in her twenties, she felt she was still "malleable enough." She said, "I was still in contact enough with the heterosexual world and that whole side of me that responded heterosexually that I could possibly have made a choice. However, I didn't, because I felt that there was something fundamentally a part of my essence that I had to honor, in my own psychological health. And even though I could play out this other game, I really needed to be true to myself. . . . Socially, I could have been heterosexual. Psychologically, I think I have always been homosexual. I've always been a lesbian. And the choice for me was to honor that."

Several interviewees felt that there was no choice involved in being a lesbian—neither for themselves nor for others. Wendy Hammond, Susan Becker, and Deena King all felt that there was no choice. Susan argued, "People are what they are, or they can choose to try and be different from what they are, but they aren't. I think eventually they come back to what they really are." Deena felt that there is a biological basis to homosexuality. "I believe it's genetic. I don't have anything to back that up, you know, but in my heart, I believe it's genetic. I think there are women that can go through a certain amount of experiences in their life that may throw them into that path, but I think deep down, somewhere, it is a genetic seed of some sort that creates that. . . . You could have the gene, and not act upon it. As well as I think you could not have the gene and maybe try to act upon it. But I think you're more comfortable if you have the gene and you're acting upon it."

Others were equally adamant that they chose. Chrissy Herek was certain that it was a choice for all women: "It's not something I was really born with or anything." For Laurel Jameson and Leslie Mohr, too, their sexual identities involved choice. Even though others might not experience their sexual identity that way, they themselves felt a degree of volition. Laurel felt that this may be especially so for bisexual women, "because we are so in-between."

Honoring the Self

For many women, to embrace a lesbian identity is a way of honoring the self. Unlike earlier images of lesbians as "sick" or "perverted," this image of lesbianism is one of self-determination and freedom—of enhanced self-esteem and well-being. Although there are clearly those who are not comfortable with a lesbian or bisexual identity (e.g., Anne Biersmith), and there are those who have struggled for years to become comfortable with their identities (including Wendy Hammond), there are many others who see their sexual identity, whether chosen or not, as a form of self-love and self-affirmation.

Joan Borman describes a moment of realization that occurred while reading a poem by Adrienne Rich, in which Rich talks about "always wanting the twin, equal with powers, equal to our own. I understood immediately that I was going to have to leave this man. I mean, it was at that point that I said, 'Oh, my God, that's what this is all about.' You know, my whole life I have wanted to have somebody who was I felt *up* to me. I don't even know what that meant, you know, but *up* to me. And these guys have not been up to me, and I need to get out of that situation." Coming out as a lesbian "led me to being with women as a way of not just feeling in control of my life, but feeling alive."

Later, she remarked, "I said to someone just the other day, 'If I were someone who prayed every day, I would be very thankful. I would give thanks every day that I am not a straight woman, but that I am a lesbian.' I really feel that my life is just, well it just blossoms. . . . I've gotten to do so many of the things that I couldn't even imagine wanting to do [if I were heterosexual], 'cause there was no room to begin to imagine doing them. And I am delighted with being a lesbian. I think it's great."

Ilene Zemke echoed Joan's sense that the men she knew were not her equal. "I saw every woman in my family as someone who I admired and wanted to be [like], from my grandmother to my mother, to my older cousins, second cousins. And I made a vow to myself as an early teenager that I would not want to be in a situation where I was in any way being told what to do by someone who I didn't respect to be at least as good as I was in every one of those categories or better. And I sort of forgot that during those periods of time . . . of being active as a heterosexual woman. I kind of put that on hold, just let myself do that little heterosexual number, but then that came back to me. And it came back very strongly that the people who I have admired in my life were women."

Denny Slater saw being with men as "self-abusive." In contrast, being a lesbian has for Denny "been a journey to be myself." The most important thing, she said, "is the opportunity to have trust with a person and to fly with that, the soaring. . . . It's given me more energy, and it's given me respect of self and respect of other human beings. I can be gentle. Because I think sexuality and being intimate opens a lot of doors to old fears, and I think that that's good. It may be scary, but it's good. And it's good for my personal development."

Community Contexts

The meanings of lesbian and bisexual identity are shaped by the social and historical contexts in which lesbians and bisexuals construct their lives and their identities. In her study of British lesbians, for example, Celia Kitzinger (1987) identified five identity accounts, including a radical feminist identity, a transitional identity, a "special person" account, an individualistic account, and an account that sees lesbianism as a path to personal fulfillment. There are clearly similarities in our two studies. Kitzinger's account that stresses lesbianism as a route to personal fulfillment, for example, is somewhat analogous to this study's account stressing the importance of social and emotional relationships with other women; and Kitzinger's bisexual account also bears similarity to the third account in the present study. But there are also differences, which may result from the different historical, political, and regional settings in which the two groups of women construct their sexual identities and their lives.

While lesbian life in the United States is in many respects similar to British lesbian life (e.g., both have well-developed lesbian/gay political movements), there are, of course, regional differences in the development of lesbian/gay/bisexual politics and communities. The women described in this study are from a small city located in a primarily rural area; in contrast, over half of

Kitzinger's sample came from a large urban area (London, England). Because her sample is more heterogeneous, we would expect somewhat different (and perhaps a larger number of) accounts to emerge. Kitzinger describes a more radical separatist segment of the community than I found. Although there is a strong feminist group in this community, it tends to be centered loosely around those who are involved in women's studies in one way or another. There are other feminist groups as well, but there is no longer a strong radical separatist core in town.[2]

Nonetheless the community I studied and many of the women in it were heavily influenced by the contemporary feminist movement. The community itself grew enormously during the 1970s and 1980s, and many of the women came out as lesbians in the context of that movement. Because of the way in which lesbian feminism conceived of lesbian identity, it is not surprising that all of the identity accounts identified in this community downplayed the importance of sex and highlighted the importance of social and emotional relationships with other women.

A study of women less influenced by the feminist movement would likely yield different identity accounts. For example, in some urban areas during the 1980s and 1990s butch-fem sexuality has experienced a resurgence (A. Stein 1992a, 1993; Nestle 1992). Butch-fem lesbian identities, in contrast to lesbian-feminism, may arise out of a more sexual definition of lesbianism, at least according to some (McCowan 1992). By 1994, a small number of women in this community had begun to think of themselves in this way. Even so, the new butch-fem styles seemed rooted in a feminist analysis of sexuality (e.g., Nestle 1992). Joan Borman, for example, had begun to reclaim a sense of herself as an "aggressive fem." As she said, "I like dressing. I learned it from my mother. It's very clear to me it's a big part of my identity." But gaining pleasure from costume, from dress, is not at all at odds with a strong feminist activism.

Although butch-fem lesbians describe and experience their sexual identities in a variety of ways (see Nestle 1992, 1987), part of butch-fem sexuality entails identifying with "masculine" or "feminine" aspects of the self. For butch-fem lesbians, erotic attractions to other women may be based in large part on the attractions of difference. Unlike in the 1950s, when women who chose butch-fem roles engaged in relatively strict codes of behavior (see Kennedy and Davis 1993; Davis and Kennedy 1986; Faderman 1991), 1980s and 1990s butch-fem roles seem more fluid and loosely defined. But just as lesbian feminism never became the dominant form of lesbian identity, it is unlikely that butch-fem lesbianism will become dominant either. Rather, it is likely that a number of different conceptions of lesbianism, some based more on sexual attraction than others, will coexist.

3

Changing Selves

Coming-out narratives often sound like religious conversions.[1] These stories, often surprisingly similar, sometimes sound like this: "Once I was lost (closeted, trying to be heterosexual), but now I'm found (lesbian). As a pseudo-heterosexual, my life was full of pain and trauma. Now, as a lesbian, even though times may be hard, I have found my true self."[2]

The moment of coming out is an epiphany. New friends circle round to witness the event. As in religious conversions, the past is reconfigured in light of one's current salvation. Past heterosexual acts, feelings, and behaviors are interpreted as unpleasant or indifferent; if enjoyed, they are sometimes reconstructed as diversions from the lesbian path or as false consciousness. Every past lesbian inclination, every kiss of a woman that almost happened but didn't, every crush, every significant or even insignificant relationship with a girl or woman is interrogated for its indication of an unbroken lesbian path leading from one's childhood or adolescent past to one's lesbian present. In this way, many lesbians come to an understanding of their current identity as stable, unchanging, or, at most, changing only once: from heterosexual to lesbian.

Clearly not all lesbians experience their identities in this way. But the experience of coming out, for many, is a kind of "coming home." Many women do, in fact, remember their earliest sexual identities as lesbian (or as "pre-lesbian") and experience coming out into a particular community or relationship as a way of finding their "true selves." Some women truly feel that they were born lesbians, and though they may have tried to live as heterosexuals, such efforts were doomed to failure. These "true believer" or "true self" narratives seem to fit with prevailing accounts of identity. That is, seen as essential, unchanging parts of the self, lesbian identities are commonly described as discovered, not created or performed.

As social constructionist accounts of identity predominate within the academic world, lesbian and gay political activists in what is typically counterposed as the "real" world increasingly present the argument that lesbian/gay identity is an essential and fixed attribute of the self. But even the staunchest social constructionists don't typically examine changes in sexual identity over the life course. With the exception of a recent upsurge of interest in bisexuality (see, e.g., Rust 1992a, 1992b, 1993; Weinberg, Williams and Pryor 1994; Garber 1995; Klein 1993), relatively few have considered such changes. Even discussions of bisexuality may be constructed as "true self" narratives. Carla Golden (1987, 1994) is one of the few who have taken seriously the notion of sexual fluidity.[3]

While for many—perhaps the vast majority of people—sexual identity is essentially stable, for others, it is not. But the experiences of this latter group of people tends to be obscured, in part because of the methods we use to research sexuality. Most empirical studies of lesbian or gay identity have been conducted at one point in time. If we ask people about their coming-out stories or ask them to describe their current sexual identity and how they came to it, their stories will typically reflect wherever they are at that particular moment. This should not be surprising: people's accounts and stories tend to justify whatever actions they've taken. If you ask people about other important aspects of their life—decisions to become a parent or not, to move to a new part of the country, to enter into a relationship—their stories of how they came to that decision and how they feel about it will inevitably reflect the choices they've already made. But people's lives don't remain on a predictable path: They gain new information, they change their minds, or other events happen that impinge on a particular decision. If we ask people later on about the same life event or decision, their retrospective stories may be different.

Sexual identity is no exception. If we ask people about their sexual identities at varying points in time, we begin to see a different picture. In discussing sexual fluidity, however, we need to keep in mind that sexual identities are, basically, labels that individuals attach to themselves, and they may or may not be closely related to behavior. Some who have called themselves lesbian but find themselves in relationships with men continue to think of themselves as lesbian (see Holly Near's 1990 autobiography for one well-known example). Others use the opportunity to reassess their identity.

Changing Partners: Getting Married, Dating Men

When Sally Zimmerman was first interviewed in 1989, she was in the process of ending a long-term relationship with a woman. At the time, she called herself a lesbian, and she had thought of herself in that way for ten years. As she related her coming-out story then, "I knew that I was a lesbian when I was twelve. But I didn't know what to do about it. So it was sort of this strand that went through my life. And I was married [to a man] when I was nineteen, so I was married for seven years. But there was still this part of myself that was a lesbian that I didn't quite know what to do with. So I came out when I was twenty-seven. And started calling myself a lesbian at that point." Sally came out into a feminist, activist network of friends, and she continued to be active in lesbian and progressive politics over the years. Although she had been married, she emphatically did not think of herself as bisexual, calling the time when she was involved with both men and women a "bisexual phase" prior to assuming a "real" or "true" identity as a lesbian.

By 1994, Sally's life circumstances had changed dramatically. After she and her partner broke up, she did not get involved with anyone seriously. Dating women seemed difficult, and she didn't connect strongly with anyone. She bought a house, which she thought would bring stability for herself and her school-age daughter, and had pretty much resigned herself to not being involved with anyone for a while. "I really thought, 'Oh, I'll never be involved with anyone again.' You know, the lesbian community [here] is so small, and you know I knew everybody, and everybody knew me."

Then, quite unexpectedly, she found herself attracted to a man who lived in her neighborhood and who had become a close friend. "And I thought, oh my God. This isn't what I thought I was going to do. . . . I mean, it wasn't that I ever said I wouldn't, but I just never imagined that . . . that would be something I would want to do." The more her friendship with this man, C., deepened and developed, the more it became clear that they both wanted to become involved. And so, with a great deal of trepidation on Sally's part, they did. Six months after Sally and C. became involved, they were legally married in a Quaker-style ceremony at their home.

A comparison of Sally's identity account from 1989 and 1994 shows both consistencies and contradictions. In her first interview, Sally had defined what it means to be a lesbian fairly broadly—especially for *other* women. At the earlier time, she said that being a lesbian means "I'm a woman-identified woman. For me, it means that I am sexual with women." At the same time, however, she said, "I don't have a problem with other women defining it differently. I have several women friends who have been lesbians and are now with men, or who have never been with women but are so woman-identified that they're just dykes, you know?" While others who had the same experiences might call themselves bisexual, in 1989, she did not. In the earlier interview, she described a time in her early twenties: "I was seeing men and women and calling myself bisexual, but knowing that I really was a lesbian and sort of had to go through that phase. For me [bisexuality] was a phase; it's not a phase for everybody."

By 1994, her self-definition had changed fairly dramatically. In the second interview, she used a number of terms to describe herself: bisexual, queer, a lesbian involved with a man, *not* straight. At base, she said, "I'm not a straight person, whatever that means. . . . I mean, I still have people ask me if I'm a lesbian. But I'm a lesbian that's with a man." She has also begun to like the word *queer*. At an earlier time, she had felt that the umbrella term glossed over important differences. "Now it feels to me like it kind of helps in some ways some of who I am, which is not straight. But if I say I'm a lesbian, I'm afraid that I'm floating on someone else's coat tails, 'cause I have the privilege of being with a man."

Sally now sees sexuality more as a continuum and suspects that more women who currently identify as lesbians will eventually become involved with men. Her understanding of sexuality as a choice and as changing over the life span has expanded. At the same time, she finds others uncomfortable with her sexual fluidity. "The culture's laid out these notions about what you have to be, and it's either/or. . . . People, I think, are real uncomfortable with the notion of, well, what do you mean? A little of both?"

Sally's account is interesting in that she uses "true self" narratives to describe her identity at both points in time, even though the nature of her identity has changed. In 1989, she described her "true" identity as lesbian. As she put it then, "It's who I am! And for me, to live my life as who I am is the only way to do it. I have to live true to my heart." Even though she had had significant relationships with men, she discounted their relevance. As she described in 1989, coming out as a lesbian did not feel wholly a choice: "The consequences for me for not choosing to be lesbian were greater than I wanted to pay. . . . It just didn't feel right." In the second interview, Sally used a similar "true self" account to describe what she now thought of as her essential bisexuality. In this interview, she said that she had "always" known, at some level, that she was "essentially bisexual," but recognizing that was difficult because she had "such a home in the lesbian community." Early in the interview, she discussed how the Lesbian and Gay Task Force had broadened itself to become the Lesbian, Gay, and Bisexual Task Force. She said, "I started getting involved in the whole discussion and realized I had always known that I was essentially bisexual."

Others may experience similar changes in behavior, with far fewer repercussions for their identity accounts. Like Sally Zimmerman, Cheryl Cook was in a relationship with a woman at the time of her first interview. By 1994, she also found herself, again, in a relationship with a man. Yet in a number of ways, Cheryl's story is very different from Sally's. At no point does Cheryl use a conversion narrative to describe her experience. At the time of the first interview, Cheryl was in the process of getting a divorce from her husband, to whom she had been married nearly fifteen years. She was also in her first sexual relationship with a woman. At the time, Cheryl thought of herself more as bisexual than as lesbian, although her sexual identity was in a bit of flux. As she described it, "in terms of accepted terms, I would call myself bisexual. Now if I think of sexuality as being on a continuum, I would say I'm more of a lesbian than I am anything. But I guess my feeling is that I'm bisexual."

Although at times Cheryl leaned more toward thinking of herself as a lesbian, she did not have the same strong feelings about her sexual identity that most of the other women did, and she seemed far more tolerant of ambiguity in her self-description. At one point, she discussed her reaction to her husband's question, "Are you a lesbian?" In response, she said, "'Gee, I don't know. Maybe.' You know, 'cause I didn't know. I mean, I still don't know. . . . Like I've said to people, 'I don't know. Is there an analysis you can do? A blood test?'" Later in the first interview, she said, "I think I identify more with lesbians than anything. . . . If someone came flat out and asked me, Are you a lesbian? And it was somebody that was asking me, Do you prefer to be with women or men, I'd say, yes, I'm a lesbian. But if it were a general question, I'd say I'm like anybody else, I'm bisexual."

At the same time as she thought of herself as primarily bisexual, she anticipated then that her future relationships would probably be with women. Yet she also felt that she clearly had a choice. By the second interview, Cheryl was no longer as certain that she would ever again become involved with a woman. Although she enjoyed her long-distance relationship with a man, she remained open about the future. "I don't know what it's going to be like, you know? I'm open. I like the relationship I'm in now. It's very different from anything I've ever been in. . . . I feel I'm a real equal in this relationship. I really do. Even much more so than when I was involved with a woman. I don't feel I have the power struggle I've had in my other relationships. I'm my own person. I have a voice. I'm respected. And I have to have that in a relationship. I don't know what sex the person's going to be, but I have to have that. So if it continues, this would be great."

While Sally Zimmerman's identity account changed fairly dramatically from one interview to the next, Cheryl's sense of her own identity remained fairly consistent. In both interviews, she described herself as predominantly bisexual—as she considered most people to be. In her earlier interview, as she was trying to understand her transition from living a predominantly heterosexual, married life to one that included being involved with a woman, Cheryl said about her sexual identity: "It's pretty much been fairly constant. I mean, I've always felt that I was bisexual, because I feel that's the norm. And then you make a decision whether you want to be with a woman or you want to be with a man." Cheryl used much the same language to describe her sexuality in the second interview: "Sexuality is, in my mind, a bell-shaped curve. And . . . anyone who claims they're 100 percent gay or 100 percent heterosexual, they're the outliers here. I think by and large people are bisexual."

At the same time, Cheryl does not count her sexual identity as one of the more important parts of her identity, a stance that she has held consistently. In both interviews, she described herself as a private person, one who does not like to talk publicly about her sexuality. Nor does she think about her sexual identity very much. At the beginning of the second interview, when I asked her how she described her sexual identity, she said, "You know, until you called I have never thought about it. Because I don't define myself in terms of my sexuality. I mean, it's an important part of my life. But it's not how I define myself. So I guess if someone said, how *do* you define yourself, I would say I'm bisexual." At both points in time, her identities as a woman, a mother, and as a small business owner remain far more important than her identity as a bisexual woman.

While Sally's and Cheryl's histories seem similar in several important ways—they are both mothers, they had both been married to men, and they had had significant relationships with women at the time of the first interview—the differences are also important. One of the things that distinguishes Sally's and Cheryl's experiences is their different relationships to the lesbian community. Although both considered themselves feminist, Sally had thought of herself as a distinctly feminist lesbian. She had come out in the context of the women's movement, and she had felt embedded in and nurtured by the lesbian community. She had been active politically, and she had given many public talks about lesbian parenting and antioppression workshops from a lesbian perspective. Her feminism and her lesbianism were clearly intertwined, and her relationship to the lesbian community bolstered her sexual identity in ways that Cheryl's did not.

Cheryl did not consider that her sexual identity was related to her feminism, either in 1989 or in 1994. Her sexual identity was not at all attached to her politics, and although she had lesbian friends (at the time of both interviews), she had never thought of herself as immersed in either a feminist or a lesbian community. At the time of the first interview, she did not seem particularly familiar with the lesbian community or the people, groups, and institutions that made it up. At the time of the second interview, she felt distant from it; although she had friends within it, she did not feel included. A private person, she did not want or seek out any greater involvement in a lesbian or bisexual community. For Cheryl, sexual identity was essentially an individual phenomenon. For Sally, sexual identity was in large part a shared group identity.

Because of Sally's greater investment in the lesbian community, the decision to let herself become involved with a man was much harder for her. When she began to feel the attraction to C., she sought out the advice of a lesbian friend. "I had this tremendous sense of ambivalence. Should I do this? Should I not do this? And I knew that there was so much offered in this particular relationship. There was just something there that I knew that this was an opportunity, and I would be really foolish not to grab it. But I was really scared." Choosing to become involved, for Sally, meant coming to terms with her relationship to the lesbian community and, eventually, grieving the loss of being a part of the lesbian community in the same way. At first, she asked herself, "Am I abandoning the community? You know, all this stuff. I didn't want to abandon the community, I still needed to be a part of it, and I felt like I had things to contribute."

As her relationship with C. continued, she found herself moving away from active participation in the community, in part because of the strong negative reaction she received from others, and in part because of the difficulty she felt in moving between two worlds. "I know that some of my limited involvement with the community right now is my own doing. It's very hard to live in two places at the same time. And I think I have some pain about having had to choose." Although she thinks the choice may have been inevitable, she grieves the loss of that strong connection with other women.

On the other hand, some of Sally's distance from the lesbian community is not her own choice. Shortly after she and C. sent out the wedding invitations, she began receiving anonymous hate mail, which continued for nearly three years. Most people in the community did not react so forcefully, but still, she described a coming-out process that almost seemed to parallel coming out as a lesbian. "People didn't know what to make of it. Some people were pleased, other people were outraged." But it was "weird, because everything was flipped, you know? Who knows, who doesn't know. Where can you talk about it? How much can you tell?" Now, she sees herself as more involved in a broader, progressive community. "I have friends and connections to the lesbian community. I'm not so sure that for me it's a useful place to go for support outside of individual people. But I see myself being much more a part of the bigger picture."

For Cheryl, who had never felt strong connections to the lesbian community, choosing to become involved with a man involved much less stress. Once her relationship with a woman ended, she found herself having fewer contacts with the community, although she still had lesbian friends. "When I was in my relationship with J., I had more contact because she was very much part of the lesbian community. I never felt like I was a part of it. But you know, I met a lot of interesting people through it, so that was fine. So once my relationship ended, it really dropped off." In thinking about her earlier involvement, she said, "One of the reasons I had a bit of a hard time with the lesbian community is that I always felt they wanted to wear pink triangles on their sleeves. They wanted to identify as being a lesbian, first, and then in other ways, second. And I have always felt the opposite."

Getting involved with a man, she said, is "like any other relationship," even though her friends and acquaintances don't always understand her choices. "I still have quite a few lesbian friends. It was confusing to them when I got involved with this guy. Although a number of them said that they figured I'd end up with a guy anyway. Some of them were just, some were appalled, outraged by it. And trying to figure out, what is this, what is this all about."

Moving in the Other Direction

While lesbians and bisexual women who choose relationships with men may find themselves at odds with the lesbian community, women who move in the other direction may find themselves welcomed back into the fold. Alex Goldman found herself in this position. Her account is somewhat unusual in that at both interviews she considered herself as having a "fluid" sexuality. Alex sees herself as having a bisexual orientation; yet she clearly distinguishes her *identity*, which seems to vary depending on the relationship, from her underlying *orientation*, which she experiences as bisexual. At both interviews, Alex thought of herself as having a lesbian consciousness, which persists independent of whether she is involved with a man or with a woman.

In the first interview, Alex described the development of her lesbian, feminist consciousness while in her late twenties. At the time, she became involved with a woman and, after an initial period when she thought of herself as simply "exploring" a relationship with a woman, immersed herself in a feminist lesbian com-

munity. "I became very radicalized. . . . I was completely identified with the lesbian community—with lesbian literature, music,
theory, you name it." The relationship lasted six years. When it
ended, Alex moved from the area. When, single, she arrived in the
present community, she fully expected to become involved with
the lesbian community. Yet her first years in the new lesbian community were not easy ones; for various reasons, she had problems
connecting with others, a difficulty she attributed to her single status. At the same time, because the community is relatively small,
there was not a large pool of potential partners, and while she eventually became involved with a woman for a brief period, the relationship was not long lasting. Some time later, she became involved with a man.

At the time of the first interview she did not call herself a lesbian. In 1989, she said, "My latest distinction is this: I am not a
lesbian by behavior, currently, 'cause my sexual behavior is not
with women. But I coined a new idea, which is, I think I have a
very lesbian consciousness. . . . There's a certain way you think,
there's a certain way you look at things, there's a certain way—you
know, being on the margin like that just makes you respond to the
environment in a particular way, and just because you're involved
in different sexual behavior doesn't mean you lose that whole consciousness." Although she talks about the term *lesbian* as being too
rigid to account for her sexual fluidity, she also seems to have identified as a lesbian at an earlier time. When she first became involved with a man, for example, she said, "I was very adamant that
I was still a lesbian." At the same time, she said, "When I . . . came
here, I felt like it was very definitely a choice—that I could either
be with men or be with women."

For Alex, sexual identity is tied up with specific relationships.
As she expressed it during the second interview after she had again
become involved with a woman: "Somehow I feel more comfortable with saying I have relationships with women [than calling

myself lesbian]. But I don't know—you see, to me it's so condi-
tional upon who I'm involved with. . . . I have been involved with
men, so technically speaking, I guess you could call me bisexual.
. . . Technically speaking, my orientation is bisexual, but I'm involved with a woman and therefore for all intents and public purposes I'm a lesbian. But yet, but yet, it's not—how do I say it? . . .
For some women, it's a natural, right out there, prominent piece
of who they are. And I guess how prominent it is [for me] is really
fluid. . . . In certain situations, it's really prominent. But then in
others, like in this community, people are cool, people are open . . .
so then it doesn't become a central piece of who I am."

During both interviews, Alex remarked that she was quicker to
sexualize relationships with men than she was with women. At the
same time, she finds relationships with women emotionally far
more satisfying. "I like to connect really closely with people. And
one end you can connect is with emotional intimacy, another ave-
nue is through sexual intimacy. And I always [connect] with people first, particularly women, through emotional intimacy." With
women, she finds that she often waits for the other to make the first
move. In talking about her current lover, she recalls, "In getting
to know her over a period of eight months, I just was interested in
who she was, drawn to her, and I was very satisfied by the richness
of what she offered as a person. Guys usually offer half that, if
you're lucky, and part of what is interesting is the sexuality."

Now that she is again involved with a woman, she feels that she
is far more accepted by the lesbian community. "When D. and I
started going out, I was delighted at the way in which I would get
reconnected with, reintroduced to, the lesbian community." Once
people in the community began seeing them out together, "I
sensed that people were sort of approving. . . . I sensed that people
were pleased. That I was being brought back into the fold." A
monogamous person, Alex wants to remain involved with D. for
the foreseeable future. But if something should happen, if they

should break up, she does not want to get involved with men again, although she doesn't entirely rule out the possibility. When she looks ahead to the next four or five years, she sees little change in her life.

Becoming Celibate

While some women changed partners during the period between 1989 and 1994, others became nonsexual. A few began to think of themselves as celibate, whether in the context of a longstanding relationship with a woman or in the context of a long period of singleness.[4] One woman, Louise Pratt, began to think of celibacy as defining her sexual identity. She first began to talk about using the term "celibate" to describe herself during the first interview in 1989. Sexuality had always been a relatively unimportant part of her identity, and it had been a number of years since she had been involved with a woman. At that time, she said, "I feel no qualms about saying I'm a lesbian; however, I think I'm celibate might be a more appropriate term. . . . I've only in the last few years decided that celibate would be a more appropriate description. Of course, since I decided that, nobody has asked. I've not had a chance to declare myself as that at all. So I guess that makes me a closet celibate!"

At the time, Louise still identified some with the identity *lesbian*. For her, it meant "that I identify with women and I prefer the company of women, and if I'm going to be sexual I prefer to do that with women." Perhaps reflecting her growing sense of herself as celibate and her increasing disenchantment with lesbian relationships, Louise talked about becoming and being a lesbian in many, often contradictory, ways.

At one point, Louise used a true self narrative to discuss how she came to adopt a lesbian identity. Her first encounters with other lesbians during college sparked a redefinition of herself. "I defined myself as a lesbian before I was ever physically involved with a woman at all. . . . You know, some things happened in my life, and I [thought], ah hah! That makes all the sense in the world! You know, here's a new perspective on life. . . . Lots of things fell into place, and I said, 'Oh! I must be a lesbian.'" Then, in looking back on her childhood and adolescence, she said, "It all became very obvious. . . . I mean, I always fell in love with my teachers, I always fell in love with my camp counselors, I always had a crush on a woman. And I never grew out of that."

At the same time, Louise sometimes wondered if she really was a lesbian. "There's probably a repressed straight woman inside of me trying to get out, you know?" But at the time, she answered the question of her lesbianism affirmatively. "I wonder just what it is that sets me apart, and how do I really *know* that I'm a lesbian. And the criteria that I have for that is, I can walk across campus, catch eyes with someone, and we smile at each other. And I say 'Um hmm. There's one.' . . . It's just the sense of being able to pick other women out of the crowd with whom there's an affinity and with whom, you know, there's just that vibration that you can pick up." She talked about the kind of woman to whom she was sexually attracted: "short hair, aviator glasses, sunken cheeks—I go for the gaunt look . . . hook, line, and sinker. I'm gone."

At the same time that she was "sure" that she was lesbian and that her past adolescent and childhood selves could be constructed as "true" lesbian selves, she also believed that she chose to be a lesbian. She sometimes also believed that her decision to be a lesbian "was as much a decision not to be involved with men as it was to be involved with women." But even then, in 1989, Louise maintained a tentative openness toward men. She believed that "if a wonderful, warm, generous, sweet man walked into my life—in an hour. If I could manage it, you know, I would be really open for a relationship with him. I don't expect that's gonna happen. But I'm open to that."

By the time of her second interview, Louise had begun to think of herself as not having a sexual identity, or if she did have one, it would be celibate. Whatever her sexual identity was, it was distinctly *not* lesbian. In the intervening period between the two interviews, Louise had had a relationship with a woman, now ended, that was for the most part nonsexual. "I've decided now that if anyone asks me to define myself by my sexual identity I will simply say I'm celibate. It has also occurred to me that I may be interested in getting involved with a man. That is, I wouldn't rule that out. Whereas many years ago, I think I would have. So I guess that's where I am. I've been thinking about celibacy, and I've been thinking about men, you know, and just kind of thinking about it. And wondering how, if ever, these issues will be resolved. Because I really don't get along with men." When asked if she would think of herself as a lesbian these days, Louise very quickly said no. "Nor would I think of myself as straight. Nor would I think of myself necessarily as bisexual."

For Louise, thinking about herself as celibate has spiritual dimensions. Most of her life, she has felt different from others because she has had very few intimate, sexual relationships. "Why do I choose *celibate* rather than *bisexual*? I guess because celibate feels like a better fit for my lifestyle, which is in many ways monastic in terms of the quiet and the solitude that I choose. There's probably a part of me that's always wanted to be a nun."

At the time of the second interview, Louise had begun to recast her former identity as a lesbian and her earlier relationships with women. She no longer sees a lesbian identity as a "true" self—or as any aspect of herself at all. Instead, when she reflects on her earlier relationships with women, she now thinks they were, essentially, a search for a mother. "I think my involvement with women was always more emotional than it was sexual. In terms of what I wanted was the closeness, and the nurturing, and the being held." She asks, "How do you be sexual with someone who you're really thinking of as your mother?" At the same time, while she remains open to relationships with men, she asks: "How can you imagine being involved, sexually involved with a man, when you think all men are jerks?" She concludes, "I guess sexuality in general just is really alien to me."

As she increasingly comes to identify herself as celibate, the lesbian community becomes increasingly uninteresting to her. Although she has attended a few lesbian events, she feels disengaged and alienated. She still has lesbian friends. But she recognizes "that a lesbian sexual identity is not necessarily what I want. Or what I need or what I'm looking for. And it's not fulfilling me. . . . As I do that, I'm feeling distant from the community at large."

Louise has told relatively few people about her changing identity. Most still assume she's a lesbian, and she fears "coming out" as a nonlesbian would jeopardize friendships. She's not certain how much people's friendships with her are contingent on their belief that she is a lesbian. At one point, she casually mentioned to a friend that she was wondering what it would be like to be with a man. The friend—"somebody I really valued"—said, "Don't turn straight on me." Another friend, however, recently remarked that she wasn't certain if she was a lesbian. Louise responded, "That's nice, neither do I." She was relieved that she could say that and receive some validation for questioning a lesbian identity. At the same time, she knows very few people she can talk about this with—at least right now. "I'm sure I'll get to a point where I'll just say fuck 'em, you know? And if it comes up, I'll just, you know, be my revolutionary self and say this lesbian shit is not for me."

Louise's identity account is atypical. Other women incorporate a sense of themselves as celibate—either as a long-term life choice or as a temporary phase—along with their lesbian identities. Kate Williams is one such woman. At both interviews, Kate had a clear sense of herself as a lesbian. For her, being a lesbian is an essential and unchanging core of her identity. She has no doubt, regardless of her relationship status, that she was born lesbian and will always be so. Although she believes that "Kinsey was right" and that the vast majority of people are bisexual, she is not one of them. "I clearly am not interested in sex with men. And it's real basic with me. I don't like the smell of men. That's real basic with me. I do not like the smell of semen. . . . So that's something I have no control of."

At the time of the first interview, Kate was single "by choice," because she was "doing some work" on herself. By the time of the second interview, Kate was involved with a woman, whom she called her domestic partner, although they were not at the time sexually active. Kate describes getting involved in the relationship: "It was the first time I felt, gosh, I really feel good about myself. I think I'll stay single the rest of my life. I have friends. They're very important to me. And then I met A." They began seeing each other and, within the space of a year, moved in together. After a few years of renting an apartment, they bought a house. But they have what Kate describes as a "unique situation." "We each have our separate bedrooms and our own bed. And we sleep with each other when we both want to, not when just one wants to. . . . We have our own private phone lines. . . . We actually have separate lives, but common lives."

As she approaches fifty, Kate has begun to enter menopause, and she has been experiencing a number of health problems. One of the side effects, as she describes it, "has been a lack of interest in sexual activity, which has really surprised me. 'Cause I have always been someone who's loved sex and experimentation." She hopes that at some point her interest in sex will return, and she feels guilty about not wanting to have sex. But "for right now, it's just not something I'm interested in. It's a level of intimacy I'm not willing to do, to be involved in right now." Although her partner is not at the same stage and would prefer to be sexual together, she respects Kate's choice.

This period of celibacy within her relationship has very little bearing on Kate's sexual identity. She is currently calling herself "a political lesbian, but not an active lesbian, even though I'm in a relationship which has agreed on this [celibacy] within the last year." Being a political lesbian means "I talk about what it's like to be a lesbian, I try to educate people around what lesbianism is. . . . I refuse to deny that I'm a lesbian." When a heterosexual friend challenged her, asking her how she could be a lesbian when she was not currently sexual, Kate argued that when heterosexual people are not in relationships or having sex, they still think of themselves as heterosexual.

How long this period of celibacy—or this domestic partnership—will last is uncertain. Kate hopes that her sexual desire will return soon after surgery that has been scheduled for the near future. Whether her relationship will continue is another question. Kate said, "In my life I see two roads, and I don't know which one I'll take. One will be that I will continue to be in a stable relationship, and we will continue making these mortgage payments and continue grounded in our home. . . . Or I will come to a conclusion that I don't want to be in a relationship, that I want to be open and have relationships when I want to have them, with whom I want to have them. Or have ongoing long-term relationships, but we don't live together. I still see that could go either way in my life. I have no idea which way it's going to go. A lot of it's going to have to do with how honest I am with myself, and how brave I am. Or am not." Either way, it's extremely likely that she will continue to think of herself as a politically active, born-that-way lesbian.

Ilene Zemke also thinks of herself as primarily celibate within the context of a long-term marriage relationship to a woman. Like Kate, she does not see her sexual activity as having anything to do with her identity as a lesbian. Ilene and N. have been life partners for over thirteen years. At the time of the first interview, Ilene specifically wanted to talk about sex because she felt her experiences might be common but that other women don't feel safe or comfortable talking about it. As Ilene phrased it in 1989, "I am not a very sexual person. I'm not a very highly sexed person." In past relationships, her lack of desire for frequent sexual activity was a problem for her partners, which made her feel abnormal, a "freak." In her relationship with N.: "All I can say is that I've never been so happy as I am now, because it is not an issue. For me, the essential thing for being happy in a relationship is to not have sex be used as a reward or withheld as a punishment, and to not have there be any discussion of sex, in terms of when are we going to do it."

Ilene is clear about her priorities: "I couldn't live without kindness. I couldn't live without love being shown to me. . . . I couldn't live without tenderness and without frequent, that is, daily, expressions of love and cherishment, if that's a word, and a desire for someone to be with me, and to be my friend, and to be my lover, and to love me. But I could live happily for the rest of my life without any intimate genital contact."

Ilene feels that she is probably not alone in this feeling, but that few women dare to talk about it. "I've never heard anyone really discuss sex very honestly. I've never heard anyone speak for my life. And I think it's important to say at least there is one other person out there, who identifies as a lesbian, who is in a long-term relationship, who calls a woman her lover, and is called lover in turn, and neither of them discuss, 'Well, it's been x months since we've made love.' Because we consider nongenital contact making love, and we just don't have to talk about it anymore."

At the time of the second interview, little had changed. Ilene and N.'s relationship maintained the warmth, love, and affection she had spoken of earlier, and they still felt little desire for genital sexual activity. Ilene still felt herself not to be a physical or actively sexual person and thinks that in a different time period, she might have taken on a celibate role.

She talked again about the silence surrounding celibacy in the lesbian community. "I think it's the last taboo. People talk about coming out, and they talk about gender and transgender, bisexuality. I don't think people talk about their active sexuality. Or lack thereof. And in a way it's a last taboo because I don't think people feel safe. . . . There's less fear about saying you met someone at the bar, you didn't know them, you were attracted to them, you went home and you slept with them than saying you've been in a relationship with someone for x years and haven't made love for x years."

Women's experiences of celibacy are varied: They may experience lack of desire for sexual activity with another person as temporary or long-term, in the context of a relationship or alone. For a very few, celibacy becomes intimately tied up with sexual identity. For others, and perhaps more commonly, celibacy is only loosely connected with identity, if at all. How prevalent celibacy is among women who define themselves as lesbians, I don't know. Out of the thirteen women who were interviewed twice, three discussed periods of celibacy either in the context of a relationship or alone. Although others may have had similar experiences, they didn't speak of them.

None of the three women who saw themselves as celibate knew of others who felt the same way. None had felt comfortable talking about it to others. Kate was particularly worried about tape recording the conversation; she didn't want others to know that she was not being sexual in her current relationship. Yet each of the three wished for others to talk with. Even Louise, who leads a life of peace and quiet and (with the exception of a women's spirituality group) mostly avoids group activities, would have welcomed a support group to discuss celibacy.

Lesbian identities are often seen, at least by outsiders, as inherently sexual. To some—especially those among the religious Right who seek to define sexual orientation solely by behavior—the concept of a celibate lesbian is oxymoronic.[5] Among lesbians themselves, the relationship of sex to sexual identity is a contested one. With the emergence of a more openly sexual lesbian culture in the

1980s and 1990s—at least on the East and West Coasts—characterizations of lesbianism have begun to shift. A number of lesbians have recently challenged the view of lesbians as essentially asexual, arguing that lesbian feminism "desexed" lesbian identity. Debates about lesbian sexuality have flourished. (See the now-classic volumes by Vance 1984; Snitow, Stansell, and Thompson 1983; see also A. Stein 1992b.)

These debates notwithstanding, the link between sexual identity and sexual activity is not a straightforward one. Some women clearly *do* define their lesbian identities as inherently and unambivalently tied to particular sexual relationships. As Alex and Cheryl's stories seem to indicate, for some women sexual identity is tied to relationships, if not to active genital sexuality. Yet it is equally clear that for others, sexual activity is only loosely related, if at all, to identity. The ties between activity and identity are mediated by relationships to particular individuals and within particular communities. As Louise's story suggests, it is extraordinarily difficult to maintain a lesbian identity in the face of extended periods of celibacy that do not occur in the context of an intimate relationship. Were it not for the difficulties involved in "coming out" as celibate and the loss of community, even one to which she is only tenuously bound, she might have moved away from a lesbian identity earlier.

For both Louise and, in a somewhat different context, Sally Zimmerman, ties to a lesbian community and to particular individuals and friendship networks may provide support for a continued lesbian identity in the face of sexual behavior that would seem to suggest otherwise. At the same time, as Ilene's example shows, it is not at all difficult to maintain a lesbian identity within the context of a loving, intimate relationship with a woman and an ongoing (though sometimes difficult) relationship to the lesbian community.

Sexual Stability, Sexual Fluidity

Not all of the women experienced a change in either sexual behavior or identity. Most, in fact, did not. All experienced life changes of one sort or another, either major or minor. Susan Becker and her partner bought a house, and Susan, who had formerly been much more closeted, became active in lesbian and gay politics. Denny Slater and Patrice Amaro returned to school, and both moved out of old relationships with women and into new ones. Joan Borman's ten-year relationship ended, which sparked a life crisis and a major reassessment. By the second interview, she had just begun a long-distance relationship with a woman.

Leslie Mohr and Kate Foster left town for new jobs, and Kate entered into a relationship with a woman in her new community. Deborah Schmidt became a single parent. Bisexual activist Laurel Jameson was no longer a lesbian "virgin," but by the time of the second interview she was still living alone in a big farmhouse outside of the city limits. For Sarah Greene, relatively little had changed. She was still single and very much a loner, although she continued to have a small circle of friends who lived in the same area and had similar interests in farming and market gardening. A number of women were nearing or entering menopause.

Whether these women experience their sexuality as inherently more stable than those whose stories were presented in this chapter, I don't know. Perhaps if interviewed earlier in their lives—or later—more of them would have discussed these types of changes. Perhaps not. How prevalent sexual fluidity actually is and the common patterns for change are clearly beyond the limits of this study. In any case, the design of this study (initially interviewing only women who called themselves lesbian or bisexual) prohibited me from examining changes in identity from heterosexual to lesbian, except as retrospective accounts. The interviews with bisexual women, presented in Chapter 8, provide additional insight.

The stories presented here hint at some of the relationships between community and identity. The identity accounts are suggestive of the ways in which communities can work to bolster—or not—specific sexual identities. Sally Zimmerman's story seems to indicate that lesbian communities invest in supporting lesbian identities, not bisexual ones. As the stories of women who have experienced change demonstrate, many lesbians are suspicious of women whose sexuality seems fluid. Perhaps the example calls up questions about their own identity. If someone like Sally or Alex can get involved with a man, these women may think, perhaps I could because our backgrounds and histories are not all that different. These thoughts may be threatening for those who believed their questions and struggles about sexual identity were settled. That for some women sexual fluidity persists in the face of such obstacles is remarkable.

4

Essentially Lesbian?

Performing Lesbian Identity

In 1989, before she began to think of herself as celibate, Louise Pratt distinguished the times when she felt most lesbian. "The times I really tune in to being a lesbian per se are the times that I get caught up kind of in the role. You know, when I see a woman in a shirt and a tie and a leather jacket. And I go wild. Or the times that I put certain clothes on, and I am struck by the effect, you know, whether it makes me feel really butch or whether it makes me feel really fem. I'm often struck by *feeling* a certain way, you know—a certain swagger when I walk, checking myself in the windows in my sunglasses and, you know, really cool . . . I'd say 'Yeah!'"

Louise described how one woman she knows puts on a lesbian performance. "There's one woman I know who—when she chooses to—can be more or less of what I identify as a classic—well, *my* classic butch. . . . Because she's really very slender and she's very meek when it comes right down to it. But when she puts on her nice pants and boots and a white man's shirt and a necktie and her leather jacket, partly zipped, and a haircut that's kinda short and her aviator glasses. I mean, I had known this woman and not paid much attention to her. But then one night I saw her at a party dressed like that. And what an effect it had on me. You know, I just said, 'Oh, my God, I'm in trouble now!' And I followed her around the rest of the night!"

It was harder for Louise to describe what might call forth those feelings in herself. "It's not like I have a specific outfit that I put on that makes me feel that way, you know, that makes me feel like I'm ready to swagger. It's just, all of a sudden it's there, and I'm in the mood, and I start to use my hands differently and start to walk differently."

Lesbian Performances

When lesbians and bisexual women present themselves to each other and to the world, they are, in effect, performing. Through these performances, they construct and reconstruct lesbian and bisexual selves. Yet the notion of play or performance does not mean that lesbianism is a role, something one can slip in and out of easily (Butler 1991). Lesbian identity is constructed *in* and *through* such performances. In this way, women signal to themselves and others the nature of their desire for women.[1]

Marcela Reyes talks about acting butch. She distinguishes between "playing" butch and "really" being butch, but acting and being are not always separated. "I have friends that I guess you would call butch, and we used to kid around because it happens to be that we both, we consider ourselves butch. And probably to some others I wouldn't be butch. But when we're together, we're both butch, and she's very tough and I'm really tough."

Marcela thinks that others, and maybe her best friend, take being butch too seriously. "As we got even closer, I realized that it is just a sort of facade, an image with us, and we play it up when we have to. We can really do it really good. I mean, if I had to protect myself, or my lover, you better watch who you're messing with. But when we're kidding around among other lesbians or dykes, . . . people know you're kidding around about it, and it's okay to joke about that. And we'll walk off with our chests inflated, . . . and we're just messin' around."

What made her wonder about whether her friend took it "too" seriously was that her friend had "some pretty sexist attitudes just because of how she was raised—the girls did the cooking and stuff like that." Her friend felt that those kinds of things were for "girlies" to do, not for herself. "But," Marcela continued, "I really think it was a role she was playing."

At the same time as she criticizes those who take the role too seriously, Marcela seems to delight in her ability to play with it. Yet she feels that there is something truly more "butch" about herself than some other women, especially her lover, R. "Like I can talk the language and I can be tough, and da-da-da. Whereas if R. tried that, she wouldn't fit in too well. If she would try that, everybody would know the minute she opened her mouth, where I can play both parts really, really well."

Part of what is interesting here is the notion of play that surrounds butchness and femness—important themes in lesbian history and culture. Both Marcela and Louise take aspects of what they understand to be butch or fem and incorporate them into their presentations of self. Yet their appropriations of butchness and femness are not wholly serious. In Goffman's (1974) terms, they are "keyed," as when "serious" action is transformed into something playful. And for each of the performances, an audience is necessary. For Louise, the audience is herself. She can tell when she feels "really" lesbian, when "it's there," as she looks at her reflection. Dress is crucial to creating that swagger, that sense of herself as "really" lesbian.[2] For Marcela, the audience is clearly other lesbians. When she and her friends walk around with their chests puffed out, they're clearly playing to and playing with other lesbians. But for Marcela, there's something "real" about the play: Even though she plays butch and crosses over between butch and fem, she still sees herself as more butch than her lover, who cannot really cross over.

These performances involve serious play. Although Marcela is adamant that she's not "serious" about being butch, the playfulness extends primarily to other lesbians. If a straight man were to call Marcela a butch dyke, she would certainly interpret those as fighting words; called the same by herself or butch friends, she puffs her chest out in pride. Too, these women are serious about their desire for women; in some sense, they are serious about "being" lesbian, even as they play with what that might mean.

Other women did not mention this same sense of play or performance. Whether they do not "play" with their sexual identities in this way—or do not consciously do so—is not clear. Perhaps some do not feel they "play" or perform *any* of their identities. But all the women interviewed have fairly elaborate notions of what a lesbian "looks like," even if they do not themselves feel they look like that, and they have a sense of whether or not they can tell if another woman is a lesbian. In presenting themselves in patterned ways—or by using these patterns to evaluate whether they "look like" a lesbian or not—the women participated in a collective framing of lesbian presence, one that relies more heavily on a coding of lesbian identity as butch. At the same time, women drew shifting and uncertain boundaries between themselves and heterosexual women. While lesbians may work at lesbian performances, sometimes these performances are expanded to include heterosexual women; other times, not.

Although Teresa de Lauretis (1991) and other queer theorists warn against seeing lesbian and gay sexualities in relation to heterosexualities, asking lesbians and bisexual women about the similarities and differences they see between themselves and heterosexual women is one way to explore how lesbians create a sense of what is distinctly lesbian. Whatever their initial response, many of the women wavered, declaring at some points that there were fundamental and unalterable differences between the two groups, and at other times seeing close connections. As they moved through the interview, they constructed and reconstructed a permeable boundary between themselves and heterosexual women.

Several of the women felt there were no essential differences between lesbian and heterosexual women. For these women, the categories "lesbian" and "heterosexual" contained far too much diversity to compare. The attempt to define what was distinct about lesbians vis-à-vis heterosexual women did not make sense, given their experiences of heterogeneity. Cheryl Cook compared the attempt to search for differences between lesbians and heterosexuals to the attempt to search for differences between women and men. "You know how when they try to study differences between males and females, and they come to the conclusion that there is more variation within [the categories] than there is between? That's exactly how I feel about women, no matter what their sexuality. That there is more variation within than there is between straight women or gay women."

Others saw the differences, if any, as rooted in the struggles lesbians engage in to define themselves. They resisted the way in which the categorization of women as "lesbian" or "heterosexual" forced them to make generalizations. In 1989, Sally Zimmerman said, "It's not that I don't see them in those categories. I guess I see them as categories of people, and then I see so many individual differences. . . . I see heterosexual women having access to male privilege that lesbians don't have. I see some heterosexual women tolerating relationships that I think they would not ordinarily tolerate if they didn't think they were going to gain by being with men in that way. And that lesbians don't have that choice."

As a graduate student, Leslie Mohr had been influenced by poststructuralist theorizing. Early in the interview, she said, echoing Butler, "To say I'm a lesbian is not to assert an identity with a stable content." But when thinking about the boundaries between lesbians, bisexual women, and heterosexual women, sne initially saw differences. "What I could say about all my lesbian friends, and my bisexual friends, is that not being heterosexual gives us a kind of slightly off-center relation to the culture as a whole that, I think, permeates the kind of jokes we make, the kinds of off-the-cuff simplified generalizations that we can make that are a kind of shorthand for a whole set of experiences. . . . There's this shared sense of looking on when it comes to heterosexual culture."

Drawing on her long experience of living as a heterosexual woman, Joan Borman said, "I think most of the dykes I know are very different from straight women. . . . I think the main difference is that when you don't deal with men as the primary way of functioning in the world, you don't have that sense of deference to them. So that even when you are dealing with them as bosses, let's say, or supervisors, you know there are certain things you have to do to keep your job. But it's not as if you really in your heart-of-hearts take them all that seriously. You just sort of have to figure out how to maneuver appropriately. There's a certain kind of whinyness and wishy-washyness that goes away."

Although they could both think of exceptions, Marcela Reyes and Bonita Brown saw lesbians as being more able to "ask for what they want." Bonita thought that lesbians are "probably more realistic, and they realize what they really enjoy. A lot of heterosexual women put up with a lot of crap they feel they have to put up with because they're women. And I think lesbians stop and say, 'Well, I don't enjoy this, so I'm not going to act like I do.'"

Bonita was one among a small group of respondents who saw the differences between lesbians and heterosexual women as fairly rigid. Chrissy Herek also saw differences, but she saw them far less positively than Bonita did. Chrissy saw that "straight" (i.e., nonbi-sexual) lesbians are less "feminine" than heterosexual and, perhaps, bisexual women. "The only 'real,' like, 'straight' lesbians that I know (and I don't know very well) just seem defensive to me. . . . [I want] always to keep my femininity." As she sees lesbians, "They just seem cold and hard, defensive." On the other hand, she sees heterosexual women as very homophobic. In thinking about the differences among women, she said, "I just wish we could all be meshed, you know? . . . I wish that there didn't have to be that [difference]. 'Cause I don't want to fall into a stereotype."

Although most of the women were hesitant to generalize about *all* lesbians and *all* heterosexual women, at the same time they felt that there was something common shared by lesbians, which some extended to include bisexual women, even if it consisted simply of a sense of being an outsider.[3] Many insisted on a distinctive lesbian presence in the community and felt that they could often spot another lesbian. Even though the interviewees did not want to assert unmovable boundaries between lesbian and heterosexual women, they did want to assert a uniquely lesbian presence and sense of style, however shifting and changing that lesbian style might be.

Playing "Spot the Dyke"

"I play spot the dyke all the time," said Laurel Jameson. But can you tell if another woman is a lesbian? "Sometimes," she answered, "but not all." Only one of the women felt that she could *always* spot another lesbian; very few felt that they could rarely or never recognize other lesbians. The largest portion felt that they could sometimes, perhaps even often, recognize other lesbians, or they felt they could almost always tell but sometimes were wrong.

Patrice Amaro believed that she could almost always tell. "I could go in that room and say, all right, who's here?" When her "gaydar" is on, she can tell. "I think that there's room for error, but there are a lot of ways to screen it out. Whichever way, it's pretty small." Ilene Zemke felt similarly confident in her ability to find other lesbians. "I'm usually right, when I think they are. An hour before I came here I was walking [downtown] and I saw two women. I'd never seen them before, and I just kinda nodded at them, as a kind of acknowledgment that I think we might be kindred spirits in some form of our identity. And they stopped me and said, 'Can you tell me where the women's book store is?' And it was just wonderful. And we stopped and talked, and I gave them directions. And so usually I think I'm right. . . . [But] sometimes I'm really wrong."

Others felt that they were no longer able to tell because the community itself was changing, along with fashions and ideals for lesbians' styles of self-presentation. Susan Becker, a very traditionally "feminine"-appearing woman who is rarely recognized by other lesbians, said that although she thinks she can tell, "It gets harder now. At one point you could tell very much because of how a woman chose to dress." In a similar vein, Deena King said, "Do I think I can tell? [I] used to be very good. Used to be *very, very* good. I'm not as good as I used to be. And I think it's because I'm getting burned out. Or it is getting harder to tell. I mean, let's face it. There used to be a uniform." More playfully, Bonita Brown said, "My dyke-o-meter is not working! A pair of Birkenstocks [sandals] does not a lesbian make!" She often finds that women she thinks are lesbian are not.

Cheryl Cook felt that lesbians who claimed they could tell were often fooling themselves. Although she could not tell if another woman was a lesbian, she said that "lesbians tell me they can tell." "I have good friends who I have known for a long time who are lesbians, and they'll debate, 'Is this person a lesbian or not?' And they're wrong a lot of times because I know the person they're talking about." At the same time, she said, many women pick *her* out as a lesbian. After she began a relationship with a woman, she realized, "I have been really naive, because probably one of the reasons I developed such good lesbian friends is maybe I looked like a dyke."

Lesbians' and bisexuals' sense of whether they can recognize others is important in several respects. It seems linked to a desire to make connections and to see more lesbians present and visible in the world. Leslie Mohr was clear that when she wondered if other women were lesbian, "It's more like I hope they are." The sense of being able to recognize others is also connected to a particular coding of lesbian identity. Only certain styles of lesbian presentation—those most classically considered butch—are typically recognized as lesbian. Even though they knew they might guess incorrectly, women rarely suspected that those who were stereotypically "feminine" were lesbian.

What a Lesbian Looks Like

> The classic dyke haircut, I think, is really short over the ears no matter where else it might be long.
>
> LESLIE MOHR

Regardless of whether they thought they could *accurately* recognize other lesbians, and regardless of whether they themselves felt recognizable to others, every woman I interviewed identified at least several cues she used to distinguish others. These fell grossly into two categories: visual/presentational and interactional signs. Some women spoke of a kind of scale, or "dyke potential." In general, women who were perceived to be in some sense "masculine" were more likely to be perceived as lesbians, whether or not they actually were.

VISUAL CUES: Although she had a hard time specifying exactly what a lesbian looked like, Leslie Mohr was very clear about the differences she saw between heterosexual women's and lesbians' appearances. "There are certain kinds of outfits that I don't think a lesbian would ever wear. And it has to do with a look that approximates femininity, that approximates culturally approved femininity."

Denny Slater is intentional about the way she presents herself as a lesbian. In 1989, she said, "I'm not one who chooses to be available to male sexual advances, so I don't dress to flaunt my breasts or my hips or my legs. I do not wear make-up. I choose to be the person I am, and I do not compromise myself. . . . I want men to know that I'm not available for their sexual prey." For Denny, not appearing available to men is a major cue for identifying other lesbians.

Ilene Zemke usually looks for interactional cues: How two women might walk close together or interact in other intimate ways. But she also looks at physical appearance and more "superficial" signs like clothing. "The flip side of it is that for every woman who I identify, who I think she is a lesbian because of haircut, clothes, walk, appearance, energy, there will be another who I'm not identifying as such because she doesn't have these characteristics. . . . You know, probably if I saw a woman in a three-piece suit, very nicely coifed, made up, very bejeweled, stockings and high heels, I would not, if I didn't know her, I would not think, 'Ah, there goes a lesbian.' But she might very well be."

INTERACTIONAL CUES: As with physical cues, interactional cues are important. Like others, Patrice Amaro observed that just as she looks for lesbians, other lesbians are also looking to identify *her*. Similarly, Joan Borman said, "I don't pretend that I can always recognize lesbians, but I do think that there is a certain sense that gets developed, of spotting your own, based on the kinds of internal-to-the-community norms that you learn. So you know I always look for pinkie rings, and I always look to see whether, if I'm walking down the street and I catch a woman's eye, you know the likelihood is that a straight woman will always turn away. . . . It doesn't mean that there aren't straight women who would not turn away, but the likelihood is that a straight woman would turn away, and a dyke would not turn away. There's just a certain sense of presence, and it's not infallible. I don't pretend that it's infallible."

Dyke Potential

"We do a DP alert, and you look at somebody that has dyke potential," said Marcela. "And I always make sure to say that word [potential], because one time I was wrong and assumed. It was not right, in spite of all the DP this kid had."

Marcela describes dyke potential: "Unfortunately it falls back into the narrower characteristics that we have as lesbians, . . . on appearance, because that's mostly all you have when you're walking around. It falls back into that narrower category, and it would be like short hair, athletic-looking body. . . . If they carry themselves assertively and confidently is a big thing. I don't know, those are just signs of DP. How they walk, their stride, everything. . . . It's not like they have to have all of these. If they have any one of these, or any combination of these, that would increase their DP."

Alex Goldman gave a long list of attributes by which she might recognize lesbians and bisexual women. Then she noted, "This is funny. There is a traditional, feminine stereotype. . . . Any degree, to the extent that a woman shows greater degrees of deviation from that stereotype, I would question her sexuality. And this is where I think it's *crazy,* because, you know, all that means is that she's deviating from the traditional female role. And sexuality is only one part of the female role."

To be lesbian is to be coded as not feminine—but masculine, one of the guys. Wendy Hammond gives an example from when she was living in the South. "I stuck out like a sore thumb. Well, I wore jeans! And I wore LaCoste shirts. I remember wearing my brother's leather flying jacket. Well, I mean, I did that for one hour. It felt like traffic would stop. Versus the women there who spent—it was everyone who was female—spent a minimum of two to three hours in the morning putting on make-up. Everyone got up at 5 A.M. to get ready for classes. I mean the amount of make-up was—I'd never seen anything like it. It was immediate, how I stuck out." Even up North, Wendy feels noticeable. "I mean physically, I look different than straight women. When I go down the hall with the women that I work with, they look more feminine. . . . I think there's almost a different sort of physique. . . . The women are built more slender. I mean, I'm built—I'm bigger. I'm big. When I stand next to the men I work with, I'm as big as a lot of the guys! . . . If one could say that a more feminine body would be more rounded or, you know, there would be characteristics of being feminine, I feel like I would err more on the side of being more masculine looking and acting."

Deena King, too, sees herself as looking more masculine; in the past, this caused her a great deal of pain. "I was just thinking about how often I got kicked out of the men's room or the women's room, when I was working in [the Pacific Northwest]. I was a police officer, and so you're wearing the uniform, and I had short hair, which I have now. But I had short hair, and you know I wore the standard uniform, so I was constantly being evicted from the women's rest room by other women because of their automatic assumption that I was male. You get real tired of that. In fact you get to the point where you don't want to go to the bathroom because you don't want to go through the hassle, or you check it to make sure there's no one else around. You know, 'cause you just don't want to go through it any more." At the time of the interview in 1989, she was no longer working as a police officer or in a job that required a uniform and felt she was no longer as identifiable as she was before.

What is interesting in these accounts is how individual women see themselves as approximating a masculine image. Certainly, not all lesbians are tall or athletically built; not all wear uniforms and have short hair. In the scheme of things, Wendy is not *really* that big; she's probably just barely above the median height and weight for U.S. women. What's important is that she interprets her size and body shape as one of the ways in which she is not "feminine" but is lesbian. Short lesbians, or lesbians who have a more "feminine" body type may interpret other aspects of themselves as seeming especially lesbian. Sally Zimmerman knows that others can't always tell about her sexuality. In 1989, she said, "I'm not a stereotypically butchy-looking person." But she clearly pointed to other aspects of herself that she thought at the time marked her as a lesbian: "I think that I look independent and have that sense of being self-reliant that I notice in other people."

"I Don't *Look* Like a Lesbian"

Several of the women interviewed felt that they did not look like other lesbians and were often not identified by others—even when sometimes they would like to be. Chrissy Herek has mixed feelings about others' inability to tell that she is bisexual. On one hand, she very strongly wants to maintain a sense of herself as soft and feminine—qualities she does not identify as being associated with lesbians or bisexuals. On the other hand, people who are important to her are unable to tell that she is attracted to women. When a woman student sent her flowers, a teacher to whom Chrissy is very close asked her if it had bothered her and said, warning her about the apparent "dangers" of lesbianism, "Well, just be careful and don't fall into traps. Be strong. . . . You know who you are; stick to your guns." Chrissy was upset. "This person who's supposed to know me the most, the best in the world, cannot pick up or identify with the fact that, you know, I'm bisexual, or maybe a lesbian."

Susan Becker is also very traditionally "feminine" appearing. In 1989, she told a story about trying to make herself visible to a lesbian couple at a cookout. "I was wearing, I think, a pair of shorts and a shirt and some earrings, make-up. I had my toenails painted red. I got there, and I saw *immediately,* I mean it was almost a physical drawing back of these two women who were there as a couple, who had a crew cut. . . . There's almost a physical withdrawing, and I've encountered it many times." Even though by 1994 there was somewhat greater acceptance of fem representations, Susan still felt invisible. She talked about a new colleague: "who's what I call a swish, like me. And I didn't pick up on her at all. Just assumed she was straight. She just assumed I was straight." It took a mutual friend to tell each of them about the other, even though Susan by that time was fairly open about herself at work.

Joan Borman and Leslie Mohr—both of whom have a more political understanding of lesbianism—work to make themselves visible as lesbians. Joan travels frequently. "And when I travel, I absolutely make a point of wearing a triangle pin, always visible. . . . It's not so much that I want to be out there doing political education, it's that I understand especially because I don't look like whatever that stereotypical notion is of what a dyke looks like. I feel certain kinds of real obligation to not use those physical realities about me as if I were passing, you know. It's not that I want to walk around with a sign that says 'lesbian' all the time, but I don't want to allow myself the illusion of thinking that the reason everything is okay and I'm not being hassled is because people are fine about homophobia."

Leslie said, "People are always telling me, 'You don't look like a lesbian,' which drives me crazy. . . . Because sometimes I wear skirts, and because I wear bright colors a lot. I wear long earrings. I have short hair, but actually, I got this haircut a couple of, well, maybe a year and a half ago, and part of the reason was because people were always telling me I didn't look like a lesbian, and that was just provoking the 'lesbian legitimacy crisis.' So I have certain outfits that I wear that I feel like are 'butch-er' than certain others. If

I'm wearing my suit jacket, or if I'm wearing my bolo tie, or if I'm wearing jeans and boots or something like that, I feel more—I feel like I look dykier. . . . If I'm dressed in a way that is kind of fashionable, people tend to think I don't look like a lesbian."

Leslie's and Joan's accounts reveal the work that is involved in constructing lesbian identities—and the seriousness with which they take their self-representations both to other lesbians and to the larger heterosexual world. Creating a plausible account of oneself as a lesbian entails ongoing attention to dress, to demeanor, and to the small details that may signal to others that one experiences desire for women. To fail to produce or attend to these cues entails the risk of invisibility. Lesbians thus cannot be understood as "natural" women. That is, if heterosexual ("feminine") women are constructed through clothing, make-up, and a shifting array of practices that condition their relationships to men, lesbians cannot be seen as simply women unvarnished. As Cathy Griggers notes, *"The* lesbian is as fantasmatic a construct as *the* woman" (1993, p. 179). Lesbian performances are *work,* albeit sometimes playful work.

Lesbian Chic

Lesbian styles are clearly changing in the 1990s—even in smaller communities such as the one discussed here. As Arlene Stein (1992b) has written, earlier images of lesbian style were "anti-style," a rejection of American capitalism and patriarchy and a refusal to use the female body in subservient ways. In this tradition, recall that Denny Slater interprets her physical presence in the world as signaling a rejection of male dominance (and, in text not quoted here, as a protest of the use of women's bodies to sell consumer products). In recent years, a very different face is being put on popular depictions of lesbianism—more "feminine," less political. This "new" lesbian image presented by the media is, as Arlene Stein describes, typically young, white, and glamorous (Stein 1992b, p. 432; see also 1992a, 1993). Unlike earlier depictions of lesbians, and especially feminist lesbians, as dour, angry, and lacking a sense of style, this new "chic" lesbian is shown trading her support group for a shopping bag. She is no longer out to change the world—only her wardrobe. That such images of lesbians appear in the mainstream media is certainly new and, arguably, reflects progress toward lesbian acceptance in a heterosexist society. Yet by focusing on lesbian chic—lesbians who don't "look like" lesbians—these new media images both distort and depoliticize lesbianism.

Only a few women saw themselves as part of this "new" image. Most saw themselves as somewhere in-between: neither lipstick lesbian nor antistyle dyke. But whatever the recent changes in lesbian style, the coding of lesbians as not feminine *and therefore in some way masculine* predominates. Because gender is seen as dichotomous—either male *or* female—lesbian presence tends to be articulated as masculine. One lesbian said that she felt she was a third gender—neither male nor female. At certain moments—browsing in the evening gown section of a department store or in other sites of "high" femininity—I am struck by flashes of insight into this position. But the conscious articulation of lesbians as something apart from traditional notions of masculinity and femininity, a third thing altogether, is rare. At the same time, to present oneself as "butch" or "dykey" is an attempt to assert a distinctly lesbian presence that does not rely entirely on the language of "masculinity" and "femininity." Although the specific gestures draw more from traditional notions of masculinity, they are not identical (a point also made in Nestle 1992). Ultimately, the butch dyke is not a man, even if mistaken for one in the women's bathroom. And to be "too" serious, as Marcela argued, to denigrate washing dishes and doing housework as what only "girlies" do, borders on sexism.

That butch and androgynous formulations of lesbianism are more highly valued or at least more visible is not, at one level, surprising. In the context of a social system in which men are seen as the standard, and in which masculine projects, desires, and preoccupations are more highly prized, it would be surprising indeed if lesbians created an entirely different system of values. We do not make and remake our identities entirely from scratch.

The appropriation of masculine imagery, however, is not solely a reflection of masculinist bias. In creating a distinctly lesbian style, butch and androgynous lesbians define a positive lesbian presence in opposition to heterosexist notions of women as weak, passive, and small. In doing so, they enlarge the category "woman" and disrupt formulations of heterosexuality as "natural" and "normal." For some, the performance of a distinctive lesbian style allows for a kind of gender bending, a playfulness around traditional categories of masculinity and femininity. To be butch one day and fem the next, as Marcela discusses, blurs gender boundaries and highlights the artifice with which masculine and feminine subjects are created. By playing on traditional formulations of masculinity, then, butch dykes enlarge the category "man" as well.

Yet in rendering some women visible as lesbians, the creation of a lesbian presence that relies more heavily on masculine or even androgynous codings renders others as deviant lesbians, invisible to those by whom they most care to be seen. While fem lesbians also enlarge the category "woman," by disrupting the notion that feminine women are intended for men, they are far more typically seen by other lesbians as retro, if they are seen at all. Thus, there is a coercive element to the traditional coding of lesbian visibility. In drawing the circles around some lesbians—and usually excluding bisexuals—others are marginalized.[4]

Focusing attention on the performative aspects of lesbianism and the accounts that lesbians give of their performances enables us to reflect on the ways in which women draw from traditional *ac-*

coutrements of gender for their own purposes. In doing so, it is important not to miss the larger ways in which lesbian performances, as social interactions, are structured. In a recent article on "doing difference," Candace West and Sarah Fenstermaker (1995) caution that rendering a plausible account of gender, race, or any other social category is both an interactional and an institutional accomplishment. In emphasizing the ways in which lesbians signal their social presence to each other—and, importantly, obscure the social presences of some others—it is important not to miss the institutional contexts of gender in which lesbian performances occur.

5

Race, Class, Identity

"I don't tolerate people being racist. I don't tolerate people being abusive." As someone who has recovered from alcoholism, Denny Slater sees herself as "a very sensitive person" and "a very vulnerable person. . . . There's not a group of people who I don't support." But as far as identities or distinctive labels are concerned, "I don't have any of that. . . . I am who I am, and for me it's not important. I know I'm a white woman."

Born and raised working-class, Denny was doing fairly traditional (and low-paying) women's work in 1989. Prior to that, she had done many different kinds of work, including heavy blue-collar employment in all-male environments. Denny had always been careful about coming out at work and, in general, being open about her sexuality. When she thought about women who were out all the time and "in your face," she admired their bravery but felt she couldn't afford to do that herself. In 1989, she said, "If we all worked in the same place and . . . had a way of economically having resources, then go ahead. But I have to deal with the reality of, you know, someone may attack me because of my sexual preference." Unlike middle-class women, Denny had no cushion to fall back on if she lost her job. At the same time, because she had a steady income, she said, "I think that what's most important to me as a working-class lesbian is to share my economics, to share what I've acquired. I think that many women do not have economic stability as independent women. So I'm not threatened by sharing what my resources are with another woman."

By 1994, Denny had lost her job. She had been injured at work and, shortly after she returned, was fired in a way that she feels was clearly because of her sexual orientation. She used this as an occasion to rethink her life path and go back to school. She finished a bachelor's degree—again in a nontraditional field—and was considering going on to graduate school. Although she wasn't certain what kind of job she would seek, she hoped to provide a role model for other women and girls in nontraditional settings.

Denny's story hints at some of the complexities of race, class, and sexuality. Although she doesn't find labels particularly useful or important, the realities of race and class inexorably shape her social and economic landscape.

White Women Talk about Race

White women discuss race in varying ways. Some, like Krista Larrson and Susan Becker, didn't mention it at all. For these women, being white is so much an assumed part of who they are and how they are seen in the world that race, for them, is not an identity. Rather, it is an invisible backdrop against which they construct their other identities. These women do not see themselves as specifically white or European American lesbians. If asked, they would probably tell you that they were opposed to race discrimination, but they see themselves as racially "generic."

Other white women talk about race in terms of racism. Kate Foster thinks about her own identifications in terms of doing antiracist work. When asked about the other groups and identities she felt af-filiated with, she said that she felt most identified with those who do "clear antiracist, antisexist work and at the same time promote a socialist perspective."

Deborah Schmidt realizes that there are certain times when race is highlighted for her. In her daily life, she typically doesn't stop and think about her various identities: being white and middle class, a woman, a lesbian, one who grew up in a small religious sect. "I think being white is not something day-to-day that [I'm] aware of until I'm in situations where I'm thinking about racism or I've been 'intercultural.' I've been involved with women of different cultures, different races, and so then it was more something I was conscious of."

A few white women claim a specific European American or Jewish identity, and some of them used this as a springboard from which to talk about racism. Kate Williams, for example, discussed coming to identify as Irish. She said, "I went for a long time saying I wasn't white, and I'd go to different groups saying, 'I'm not white, I'm not white.' Finally, someone at an antiracist workshop said, 'You know, you white liberals have got . . . to quit having so much white guilt.' And I went, 'My god. I haven't got any white guilt.' And then I got to thinking. I am ashamed of what white has stood for all these years." As Kate recalled, the workshop leader said, "You've got to reidentify white, 'cause if you don't reidentify, who's gonna do it? Who's gonna identify what white is? You know, the KKK?" Now, Kate says, "I'm no longer saying I'm not white. . . . I identify very strongly as being Irish."

Kate's story points to the complications embedded in white women's thinking about race. In an identity-based movement, iden-tities are typically something to claim with honor. Over the last sev-eral decades, women have reclaimed proud lesbian identities in the face of a dominant heterosexist society that sees lesbianism as sick, sinful, or more benignly, as exotic and different. In this sense, posi-tive identification is an achievement. But in the context of U.S. race relations, white identities are inextricably linked to a system of domination and oppression. Few whites claim an explicit white identity, and those who do typically do so in the context of white supremacist ideology. Understandably, white progressives who wish to challenge racism have little desire to align themselves with them.

As Kate sees it, there is nothing prideful in being white; rather, there is something shameful about whites' participation in the enslavement of African Americans and the continuing oppression of people of color. Thus, in her earlier thinking, she could not bear to think of herself as white but could only insist that she was somehow not implicated in whites' dominance over people of color. Her affirmation of Irish identity is a strategy to avoid guilt and claim an ethnicity that is not, to her mind, so laden with racial meanings.

Laurel Jameson, too, described the process by which she began to identify as a white woman. She said, "When I'm in Pennsylvania, driving through Pennsylvania, I see the billboards that advertise Newport cigarettes. And there are all these beautiful young people and they're giving themselves cancer. And I think nothing of it. But then I was driving through [a medium-sized Eastern city] about a month and a half ago. And I was on S. Street, going through the Black neighborhood. And there were the billboards advertising Newport cigarettes. But this time it was young, beautiful Black women who were giving themselves cancer. And my eyes noticed that. Boy, look at the hidden agenda. When I see white people, I don't notice, because it's so taken for granted. We don't see the forest for the trees, and the fish doesn't see the water. But when I see Black people, I think, oh, something different. And I thought, it's very important that I realize: this is racism. It's not Ku Klux Klan-ism, but it's racism. It's racism. To make one group the norm. . . . So I've begun to label: this is white, this is Black. This is Native American, this is Chicano. And rather than take myself as the norm and somebody else as deviant, name us all."

Laurel contrasted her recent attempts to challenge racism with her attempts to protest racial segregation during college in the late

1950s. "We had a biracial group . . . demonstrating to integrate the last segregated business, and to protest and bring attention to discrimination in student housing. . . . We white kids worked alongside the Black kids and worked so hard. We were loving and we cared. But we saw our Black friends as white people in brown skins. And we were thinking in terms of integrating people into white norms. We were totally unaware of African heritage, totally unaware of the realities of Black lives—even though we were loving and caring. It was racist because we were blind." She sees now that racism is not just burning crosses on people's lawns, it's also a part of and created by "loving, well-meaning people."

Patrice Amaro has mixed feelings about her racial identity, which she thinks about partly in terms of her movement into the professional middle class. "I'm very much a part, whether I want to admit it or not, of the educated, white, middle-class group. Although I do come from a working class, I still have some identification toward working class." Patrice's job entails educating others around issues of diversity. She has worked hard at making alliances with women of color, both lesbian and nonlesbian, but she is respectful of group boundaries. "I can't say well, I'm a part of whatever. Because that's not the reality. But when we come to political issues, I know that I have been invited in to be a part of . . . the struggle. But that does not make me necessarily a part of that community, as much as I'm one of the safer people because at least I don't actively try to oppress people."

All of the white women who had thought about race and racism and tried to find alternate ways of thinking about themselves and their identities were activists, or had been at one point in their lives. One was part of a feminist collective; two others were active in the Lesbian, Gay, and Bisexual Task Force. Their narratives point out the difficulties posed by white women's thinking about race. Kate's protestations notwithstanding, they struggle with guilt and shame attached to being part of an oppressor class. As women, as lesbians, they try to reclaim and value stigmatized identities. Not so as whites. As white women, they try both to distance themselves from those whites they perceive as racist and oppressive and to recognize that they are not, themselves, a part of communities of color.

Not all women who claim a particular white ethnic identity do so as part of a conscious effort to challenge racism (see also Waters 1990). Cheryl Cook claimed a German identity, but she thought about it more in terms of how it shaped her personality than anything else. "I'm a cultural Catholic. And I was raised in a very, very strict Catholic household. I'm German. And I'm *very* German; I'm very hard headed."

Others argue that race doesn't matter. In an attempt to be color-blind, they end up ignoring the realities of racism. Deena King remarked, "I'm white, so I kinda have to identify with that group, though I don't have a color issue. I don't—that's the lowest on the list. I mean, I don't really see Black or white . . . You know, when I'm filling out a form I have to say white." Later, she said, "I believe in everyone being allowed the same level of freedom, and I think that no matter what your sexual preference is, that you, too, are allowed that level of freedom. And we should all be able to work together." Issues of race and of sexuality, she argued, "are trivial in comparison to the other issues that are around us today, such as world peace or pollution or other things that are out there, which escape me right now. More powerful things . . . are going on, rather than whether someone sleeps with someone or whether someone is Black or white. I think these are really trivial issues and that we've got bigger fish to fry."

These white women's stories reflect a range of thinking about racial identities and racism, from a lack of conscious awareness of themselves as white, as having particular experiences in the world because of their skin color and ethnic background, to a fairly complicated understanding of their position in a system of racial stratification. Some were actively engaged in antiracist work. Others, if they thought much about race at all, paid little attention to the system of racial dominance and their own particular position, as white women, within it.

Women of Color

The women of color did not, by and large, have the luxury of thinking about their sexual identities apart from race. When asked about her identities, Marcela Reyes said, "I hold woman of color, and if I want to get specific, I would say Latino. I identify as a Latino lesbian." Marcela's Latina identity gives her connections with other people of color. She is often mistaken as a Mohawk Indian by Mohawks, and, through her encounters with them, has begun to make connections to a Native American history. "When I'm around Native Americans I define myself as Native American. It would be Aztec, because it's Mexican Indian." These identities are very important to Marcela: "because each one of them gives me a contact with a larger group of people, another group of people . . . who support me."

Marcela doesn't see women of color as forming a unified group in the lesbian community, yet, she says, "I see it happening on an individual basis. . . . For instance, there's always that connection because you're a woman of color. Almost always. Or unless somebody else is struggling with that identity themselves. Or just are tired of dealing with this color issue. Which I don't blame people for throwing up their hands at it at all. You get tired of hearing it. Even if it is for your own best interest to be shoving it down people's throats! . . . You get tired of shoving it down people's throats." When that happens, sometimes she or others she knows withdraw for a while.

Although Marcela feels most connected with other lesbians of color, her partner is a white woman, and she worries about separating too much. She believes that in a community as small as this one, there aren't enough women of color to form a large, cohesive community, and she fears criticism from whites. "At least most of my friends don't segregate, or separate themselves from . . . white people. We all interact with white people very frequently." She wishes that there were an organization specifically for lesbians of color, but, she says, "I don't think it's necessary, just because we're able to do that [connect with other women of color] on an individual basis. . . . Sometimes I get concerned that if we started something like that, people would feel like we were separating ourselves out, and that's not the case at all."

Unlike Marcela, Bonita Brown felt very isolated from other women of color, especially Black women. Bonita had only recently moved to town to go to graduate school. Her primary identification was with "Black professionals," especially writers and graduate students. At the same time, she felt cut off from the Black community in this city and perceived conflicts between her identity as a lesbian and as a Black woman. She had come out to no Black friends, either here or at home, and she was anxious about making connections with others in the Black community. "People keep saying, or I've heard that the Black community's more homophobic, . . . and I'm not taking anyone else's views, and I really haven't analyzed that for myself. So I don't really know what they are about." She worries about being rejected because she is a lesbian. "That'll become hard because you're talking about complete exclusion. Being ostracized."

Although she longed to make connections with other Black lesbians, at the time of the interview she had not yet done so. When asked if she knew many Black lesbians in town, she said, "Unfortunately, I know a few. . . . They are exponentially difficult. Because you don't know—completely different backgrounds, different expectations, you don't know where their heads are at, you don't know what they've been through. So there's not that group." For a variety of reasons, trying to make friends was extraordinarily difficult for Bonita: "Where I come from, I guess maybe because I'm older than some of them. But where I grew up it's like, you see a Black person on the street they just speak, it's understood. And here it's not." Most of the Black lesbians she has met thus far mostly interact with white women, and Bonita felt they were simply not responding to her. "And you wonder why is that. I have definitely no problem with non-Blacks, but I don't see any other group in the world that shuns their own. I don't understand it, and I won't understand it. . . . I don't understand why the need is there to separate yourself from other Blacks, you know, even on the basis of being friends. So it's very hard to make friends. Black friends."

Bonita wonders if some of her difficulties stem from class divisions in the Black community. Although she grew up in a poor family, as a graduate student at the university she finds herself on the other side of the class divide. She has heard people say, "There are townies and there are [collegians]. And I'm like, 'What the hell does that mean?' I have never considered myself middle class, and I still don't. Probably never will. And I've never had a need to separate people on the basis of class. Because I've never valued people on the basis of how they were raised. It's how they act, you know." Because she attends the university, people "already assume that you're a snob."

Bonita's isolation was probably due in large part to her newness in town and to her general shyness, yet others had similar experiences. Tanya Williams, a middle-class Black woman, noted that the only contact she had with the Black community in town was on Sundays, when she went to one of the African American churches. Apart from that, most of her friends and social contacts were white people from the University. But unlike Bonita, this was consistent with her experiences growing up. She had lived in mostly white communities, and she often found herself the only Black person at school and in her neighborhood.

Most lesbians of color who participated in the lesbian community, especially those who moved to the city to attend school, found themselves interacting much of the time with whites. Over the period of the study, there were few resources or groups specifically for lesbians of color.[1] One Asian lesbian felt particularly isolated, both from other Asian women and from the lesbian community. There are likely many others who felt excluded from the predominantly white lesbian community and felt more at home within communities of color, even if those communities were not always accepting of open lesbians.[2]

Contrasting the stories of Marcela and Bonita with those of white lesbians provides insight into some of the hidden structures of racism and white privilege in the lesbian community. White women did not feel the need to discuss how often they interacted with women of color. Nor did they worry about being perceived as segregating themselves from women of color if they did not interact in integrated groups, as Marcela did. Although many of the white women felt strongly about challenging racism both among white lesbians and in the wider community, they did not need to incorporate into their core selves a specific racial identity and they could, without penalty, simply not think about race much at all. When white women had difficulty making connections with others in the lesbian community, they did not wonder if that difficulty was connected to their race or ethnicity, but instead looked to other reasons. Alex Goldman, for example, attributed her earlier difficulties in making friends to being single, not her ethnicity or skin color.

Class Differences

Just as white identities are taken as universal, so are middle- and professional-class identities. In this community, a peculiar inversion of class meanings coexisted with a hegemony of professional-class tastes and values. On the one hand, middle-class identities were typically not spoken of with pride. A number of middle-class women felt guilty about their class advantages. Leslie Mohr, for example, contrasted her class identity with her lesbian identity. "I'm really conscious of my class position . . . because it feels like something I don't like that much. Although I recognize that I like the privilege that it gives me and I like the comfort in the world that it gives me, I feel really conflicted about even liking those things." For Leslie, one of the pleasures of lesbianism is its transgressive nature and its marginality; in contrast, to be a member of the professional class seems appallingly bourgeois.

She sometimes sees her growing sense of herself as a professional as conflicting with her lesbian identity. "Or at least I experience it as conflictual because the dynamics seem to be so different. . . . To claim my lesbianism is to work against certain pernicious oppressions that I think need to be worked against. But I keep getting reminded of the fact that I'm right inside some of those assumptions because I'm following out my little class destiny by turning myself into a professional."

A few middle-class women were intentionally downwardly mobile, eschewing the professional jobs that their college degrees could afford them in favor of low-wage, often part-time or temporary work that gave them more free time. A larger number held professional jobs in the human services that paid relatively low wages. Still others held professional jobs but were self-conscious about consumption, taking pride in not owning the accoutrements of the professional middle class (new cars, television sets, and VCRs) as part of a radical critique of the class system and women's position in it. A number were associated with a storefront food cooperative and other alternative economic enterprises.

A few professional women were critical of others' attempts to reduce consumption and avoid the trappings of suburban life. Wendy Hammond, who held a prestigious job and had a substantial income, was critical of those who chose not to ascend through the class system. She said, "I have heard that people are upset about . . . people who have more money, for example. And that bothers me, because I think that feminism is an economic issue, in great part, and I think that achieving any kind of equality will come, to a great extent, through economics. I think it's too bad that lesbians will turn down their nose at being successful economically. I think that's a mistake." In large part because of her affluence, Wendy felt "exotic" and "disenfranchised" by the lesbian community. She said, "You know, a lot of the things I do in my current relationship nobody else does. . . . I don't know other people who travel as much as we do. Or go to the places we go. Or do what we do, economically." Although she recognized that most other women cannot afford the trips and consumer goods that she can, she didn't understand why more lesbians do not "choose" a more affluent lifestyle.

The working-class women tended to talk about their class identities differently from the middle-class women I interviewed. Katie Goshen doesn't like to use labels to describe herself. A blue-collar worker in a traditionally male occupation, she simply said, "Labels are for jars." When asked to describe herself, she said, "I'm just a regular Jane. . . . I'm just a regular kind of person. Plodding along the road of life." Although she was articulate about her work, her long-time love of softball, and her analysis of how women's softball had changed over the years, she did not spend much time thinking about identities or how she might describe herself to a researcher.

A number of women came from poor and working-class families but had completed college degrees or beyond and entered the professional middle class. These women talked about class and class privilege in markedly different ways from the women who were raised middle class.

As a business woman, Cheryl Cook had little patience with downwardly mobile lesbians. But she felt that coming from a working-class background gave her an ability to cross class boundaries and interact with a wide range of people. "I can relate to working-class women. Yet I can relate to professional women, highly educated women, moms, lesbians—I mean, I just feel an affinity with all of them." By 1994, she seemed even more conscious of class divisions in the wider community and the difficulties blue-collar workers face in trying to make ends meet. By then divorced from her husband and raising a child on her own, she articulated an acute awareness of economic issues and how women's labor is undervalued.

Patrice Amaro was far more troubled about the meanings of class in her life. She discussed the "internal struggle" she faced "dealing with being educated." "I don't have any trouble being educated. I have trouble in terms of what does middle class mean to me. Because I still very much have the working-class struggles behind me, or right next to me." Patrice was the first person in her family to go to college, let alone go on for a master's degree. When she graduated from college, she worked as a department store clerk for two years, "eking out a living, which really inspired me to go back to school." But as she put it, "A lot of the middle class is new to me. I'm still struggling to find out what does that mean. I don't have some of the—what I've seen some of my other friends have—guilt, almost, about having money, or not even money as much as the privileges that come with it. . . . They had the privilege of being able to go to decent schools and colleges. For me, it was always such a struggle to get that."

Patrice compared her life now, when she sees the world "in terms of options," to when she was younger "and much more caught into the working-class way of thinking." For her, the notion of having choices translates into a responsibility to help other people. "If it's within my power in any way to help somebody who is in that trap that I used to be in, I feel a compulsion to try to help that person out." Remembering her working-class roots means that "it's real hard for me to just totally indulge in 'this is me, I got it'" and then forget other people who are struggling.

(Counter) Cultural Capital

The notion of cultural capital is useful in analyzing some of the distinctions women made in this community. As Pierre Bourdieu (1984) argues, the class structure of society is so deeply embedded within cultural practices and tastes that it appears natural. People in different classes are exposed to different material conditions, and thus develop different tastes. Class position is not necessarily conscious, a process of identification with a particular class standing, but mediated symbolically through the production of tastes and values. Some argue that there are numerous social axes on which distinctions may be created and not all of these are wholly reducible to class (Hall 1992). In this particular community, certain kinds of distinctions were clearly important: shopping at a food cooperative instead of a "regular" grocery store, using alternative financial institutions, and so on (Chapter 7 provides a host of other distinctions as well).

Unlike in "mainstream" professional-class society, to have a lot of money and to flaunt it with the purchase of high-priced consumer goods wasn't quite acceptable. Recall, for example, Wendy Hammond's feelings of "disenfranchisement" because of her wealth and her attitude toward money. On the other hand, the truly working class—and the distinctions of mass culture—were not valued either. To shop at K-Mart, to wear polyester, or to enjoy noneducational television or violent movies was not fashionable. The mixed signals regarding class and status in this particular community could be considered part of a system of "countercultural capital." The system of distinction entailed both an overt rejection of middle-class tastes and values and an embrace of many aspects of a professional-class lifestyle, including a number of the things that an advanced education encourages: an appreciation of books, a style valuing handcrafts and natural fibers, and in general a disdain for mass culture.

Having multiple identities was also a marker of status within this community. The seventy-seven women surveyed in 1990 described their identities in many ways: feminist, Jew, recovering alcoholic, farmer, Taurus. Some of the identities were clearly volitional: softball dyke, gardener, Buddhist. Others reflected social categorization, including racial, ethnic, class, and gender identities. Still other identities revolved around relationships, like lover, mother, sister, friend. Some women constructed wholly individual identities: funky/hippie, cynic, excitement seeker, "me," honest and honorable woman. Although a few women (two) chose not to list any identities, most listed between five and eleven separate identities (the median number was 10). A few listed a very large number: twelve women listed between fifteen and twenty identities, and seven women listed more than twenty.

The patterns of identification are suggestive. Notably, feminists claimed significantly more identities than nonfeminists. On average, those who called themselves feminists listed nearly thirteen identities, versus just under nine for those who did not. Activists held, on average, just over fifteen identities, versus under ten for others. White women claimed more identities (on average, 11.5) than women of color did (7.8). What these figures suggest is the use of multiple identities as a marker of status.

The privileging of multiple identities comes out of identity politics and the radical feminist notion that the personal is political. As Shane Phelan, among others, has observed, identity politics arose in contrast to more traditional class-based social movements (1989, 1994). Early feminist organizing argued for the importance of personal experience in understanding one's oppression (Redstockings Manifesto 1970). The Combahee River Collective provided perhaps the most influential and explicit statement of identity politics: "We realize that the only people who care enough about us to work consistently for our liberation is us. . . . We believe that the most profound and potentially the most radical politics come directly out of our own identity, as opposed to working to end somebody else's oppression" (1977, p. 212). The proliferation of identities among activist lesbians is an outgrowth of this style of politics. Although a number of alternate identity accounts coexist with it, a feminist, activist account of lesbianism has predominated in the production of lesbian culture (see also Chapter 2).[3]

Although it is currently fashionable (especially in queer theoretical circles) to attack identity politics, it has been enormously important in the development of communities like this one. In these communities, identities gain currency as a source of status distinctions. In the minds of at least some women, if identities are a wellspring of political struggle and a source of belonging, then having more identities surely is better. This might explain the extraordinarily large number of identities that many (especially middle-class) women in this community claimed and their zeal in producing an array of both socially patterned and individualistic identities.

As postmodern theory and politics come into ascendance, with their critique of fixed and essentialist identities, it may well be that we will see a shift in forms of countercultural capital in lesbian communities like this one. Rather than seeing identities as markers of distinction, we may see instead a refusal to be pinned down or named. Liminal identities may come into ascendance. By 1994, there were only a few harbingers of that trend. The increasing acceptance of the umbrella term "queer" and the nascent attention to transgender politics may signify the beginnings of just such a shift (see, e.g., Feinberg 1993; Pratt 1995). Perhaps the next few years will see a move toward anti-identity, with a corresponding system of values. Until that time, however, identities will remain a source of distinction—a type of countercultural capital—within this community.

6

Twelve Steppers, Feminists, and Softball Dykes

> The most important thing I need to tell you is . . . what a
> wonderful support—the women, the lesbian women. . . .
> How fast the word of mouth travels, and how supportive
> people are to help each other. . . . It's such a versatile com-
> munity, but in a moment's notice it can come together as
> one strong being, and a pocket of energy. I don't know
> exactly the terminology, it's not quite there for me, but
> it's a very strong community. We have our rifts, but the
> rifts heal. And that's tremendously important.
>
> • • •
>
> My perception of the lesbian community: It's one of the
> most difficult communities I've ever had to break into.
> . . . I used to go and hang in [the women's book store]
> and just look at the books on the shelf, hoping some-
> body would speak to me, you know? Some lesbian is
> going to speak to me any minute now. . . . I find it a
> real closed community, until people get to know you.
>
> KATE WILLIAMS

Women described the community as close yet closed, cohesive yet claustrophobic. Some women thought of the community in all of these ways at the same time. When she first moved
to town, Kate Williams couldn't seem to find a way to break into
the lesbian community. Several years later, she described herself as
at the "center" of activist lesbian life.

For Deb Smith, one of the "founders," the lesbian community
included "a whole group of wonderful women, of great variety—
covering a great variety, and a feeling that we all—somehow we
all have close to a common vision. . . . The vision has something
to do with ourselves, and then it also connects in with having—

wanting to see changes brought about in the culture. . . . And something in there about justice, too. Yes. And enjoying each other's company, having dances and having concerts and things."

Deb has been active in the community for over twenty years. One of the things she noticed most, in thinking about how the community had changed over time, was its explosive growth. Jokingly, she said, "It's grown from one lesbian, me." More seriously, she noted that at one time she might have known everyone at a dance or party, but now she doesn't, and "there are all these youngsters. . . . So that's amazing."

Lesbian Community

In keeping with lesbian feminist ideals of sisterhood and solidarity, earlier conceptions of lesbian community stressed the importance of harmony and unity within "the" lesbian community[1] (see, e.g., Wolf 1979; Lockard 1985; Krieger 1982). According to these early accounts, lesbian communities were like one big happy feminist family. For example, in her review essay published in the early 1980s, sociologist Susan Krieger referred to lesbian community as "the range of social groups in which the lesbian individual may feel a sense of camaraderie with other lesbians, a sense of support, shared understanding, shared vision, shared sense of self 'as a lesbian,' vis-à-vis the outside world" (p. 92).

In a similar, early burst of enthusiasm, Jacquelyn Zita (1981) described lesbian community as "a place where lesbians can relax; where the worry of offending straight women no longer exists; where homophobia is erased; where the women you meet share common interests, and experiences, and desires; where lesbian sensibility and erotic caring are givens. It is the place we feel at home—a radical kinship in the making" (p. 175).[2]

Accounts like these accompanied the rush of excitement many in the 1970s and early 1980s felt at discovering feminism and lesbianism for the first time. But while many lesbians felt "at home" within feminist lesbian communities (and many continue to do so), many others felt pushed to the margins, outsiders looking in at the "family" inside (for popular literature aimed at lesbians, see Lewis 1979 and Baetz 1980; for social scientific accounts, see Barnhart 1975). In the late 1960s and early 1970s, tensions arose between "old gays," who had bravely lived as lesbians in the years before the feminist and gay liberation movements, and "new gays," who were not always respectful of the dangers that women who had come out earlier had faced and the choices they had made.[3] More recently, the "sex wars" of the 1980s split lesbian communities into two often hostile camps (see Vance 1984), and lesbians of color and disabled lesbians have challenged white and able-bodied lesbians to make lesbian communities open to *all* women (Smith 1983; Moraga and Anzaldúa 1981; Franchild 1990). From the vantage point of the 1990s, the notion of a unified lesbian community seems hopelessly romantic.

The community in this city mirrored some of these broader tensions. Some women had very strong negative feelings about the community. Kate Foster, for example, had been active in the community nearly a decade earlier. But by 1989, she had come to feel that she had "very little in common with the lesbians that I know in [this town]." She said, "I feel that more than most lesbians that I know, I am very unwilling to inscribe myself in the values and beliefs and prescriptions of a lesbian community." A series of events had caused her to lose ties with groups that she felt connected to earlier; several years later, although she still maintained close relationships with individual lesbian and heterosexual feminists, she did not feel connected to the community. "I don't feel close to [any one] group because I feel there's a protection of lesbian identity through an intensely judgmental process. . . . There is some very clear prescriptive behavior that means one is either politically correct or politically incorrect. And I'm not willing to live with those kinds of boundaries."

Alex Goldman, too, had strong negative feelings about the community, at least when first interviewed in 1989. Her estrangement was due in part to her exclusion from several groups in which she was interested in participating. When she first came out, she had "this view of a lesbian utopia. . . . Now I think that's bullshit."

Relations between and among groups within the community are not necessarily harmonious. Laurel Jameson explained: "I use the phrase [lesbian community] and I realize I'm doing it with reservations, because it's not a lesbian/feminist utopia. Surprise! I'm finding that there are actually several communities, and they don't always get along with each other."

Later in the interview, Laurel talked about how her perception of the community had changed as she became more and more immersed in it: "[We'll hear] that some women are so into that twelve-step stuff, and others of us think that was a crock of shit. . . . We'll hear that this woman is really pissed off at that woman because she is messing around with such-and-such a woman. . . . We'll find that this woman is very unhappy because she just got royally shafted by another woman. And so I discovered that there's game playing going on. And neurotic behavior. Gays and bi's, lesbians, we don't have it all together. Certain separatists want us to believe that, boy, we women have it all and the men have nothing. And we're all together. And we're not. I'll discover that sort of thing. And factions arising. And the separatists are angry with the people who will make coalitions. And all that sort of thing."

In the wake of such discord, commentators have begun to challenge definitions of lesbian community predicated on harmony and unity. For many in the 1990s, including those who had been swept up into an earlier vision of a unified "lesbian nation," the metaphors of family and sisterhood are simply inappropriate for a heterogeneous community. The eruption of differences—of race and ethnicity, of social class and access to resources, of ability, and of style—calls into question conceptions of lesbian community.

But what are communities, anyway? Are they actual places where people live and work, protest and pray, shop and socialize? Or are they "imagined," constructed more by a desire to create identity, a sense of togetherness, and a shared vision for the future? Social scientists have historically defined communities as geographically bounded spaces in which groups of people live and interact over the course of a lifetime (see Kaufman 1966; Bernard 1973; and for research specifically on lesbian and gay communities, see Murray 1979, 1992; Levine 1992).

While some communities clearly have a geographic basis (see Portes and Manning's 1986 discussion of ethnic enclaves), others do not. In Kansas City, for example, runners often refer to the "running community" with no apparent sense of irony. Yet runners, it appears, are fairly evenly distributed throughout the city. There is no single neighborhood or district in which runners live and train and race, and there is no boundary that separates the running community from others. There are organizations and events, however, that bring runners together: group training runs, races, meetings to organize events. There are bagel bakeries where runners gather; specialized stores; and newsletters that pass on race schedules, training tips, race times, and gossip about the personal lives of runners. There is clearly a sense of camaraderie, a feeling of belonging, even though this sense of belonging does not necessarily persist beyond the shared activity of running.

Even for groups as heterogeneous as runners, the language of community has become pervasive. It is one of the ways—perhaps the most common one—in which people refer to a sense of togetherness or a feeling of shared purpose and identity. Lesbians, thus, are not alone in using the language of community to refer to a sense of shared purpose and belonging.

Communities, and especially lesbian communities, are best seen symbolically (Esterberg 1995; see also Taylor and Whittier 1992; McCoy and Hicks 1979). Benedict Anderson's (1983) notion of "imagined communities," while intended to theorize the growth of nations, is particularly useful for thinking about lesbian communities. Anderson argues that nations are imagined because in even the smallest, members will never know or even hear about most of their "fellow-members." Yet "in the minds of each lives the image of their communion" (p. 15). Lesbians speak of community in strikingly similar ways. We *feel* a sense of community, of shared identity, with these other inhabitants of our social space, and in so doing create a sense of community.

An Overlapping Set of Friendship Networks

The communities we imagine, however, may not be exactly the same. "The" community is actually fragmented into many smaller, overlapping social circles, or friendship networks. Wendy Hammond, for example, saw the community as a Venn diagram. Her group of friends is a "little circle inside a big circle." Louise Pratt claimed that "it's perfectly obvious there's all sorts of different segments" in the community, and Patrice Amaro felt that "we are not one community; we are many under this umbrella of a culture." Patrice saw that there was a national or maybe even an international lesbian community that included any woman who had a sexual interest in other women or was woman-identified. Underneath, there are many groups, defined by race, age, politics, region, and other factors.

Many different groups were identified as being a part of the community. Some of these groups are large and cross-cut many other groups. Softball dykes and women involved in sobriety programs (Alcoholics Anonymous, Al Anon, and so forth) seem to be the two largest.[4] Other groups are more enclosed: cliques of friends who meet to play board games, couples cliques, or cliques of single women.

Women surveyed in 1990 described their friendship networks in a variety of ways (see table 6.1 for a complete listing). Nearly 80 percent of the women said that many, most, or some of their friends considered themselves professionals. Approximately two thirds reported that their friends were academics or college professors, and about the same percent said that their friends were associated with the University. Three fourths reported that their friends were human service professionals. Friends were also likely to be long-term residents of the community (70 percent) and in a long-term relationship with a woman (81 percent). Many of their friends were engaged in political action groups (70 percent) and in twelve-step recovery programs (61 percent).

Women reported that their friends were *least* likely to be lesbian separatists (92 percent had very few or no separatist friends), bisexuals (82 percent), or were not "out" to many other people (71 percent). Their friends were also not likely to be undergraduate students (86 percent).

The picture that emerges is of a political activist but not separatist, middle-class community with a large proportion of academics and professionals. There are certainly working-class, "closeted," and nonfeminist lesbians in the area. That they do not appear in this account is, to a certain extent, a failure of the researcher in searching them out.[5] But to some degree, it is also because these women are not visible to other lesbians who claim participation in "the" community. As an example, I actively attempted to recruit women of color, working-class women, and older women. When asked if they knew of any working-class lesbians, more than one woman referred to those who had advanced graduate or professional degrees, who worked in professional jobs, but who had come from a working-class background. The current working-class women in the community (e.g., a woman who clerked in a grocery store, another who worked in food service) simply were not noticeable to the middle-class women.

Similarly, when women were asked in 1988 if they knew of any "old" lesbians, most cited the same woman—an ardent feminist in her early fifties. Joan Borman, who at that time was in her late for-

TABLE 6.1 FRIENDSHIP CHOICES

In a Sample of Lesbian and Bisexual Women, 1990 (%, n = 77)

	Many, most, or some of my friends belong to this group	Very few, none, or don't know how many of my friends belong to this group
play on a softball team	55	45
involved in team sports or organized athletics	42	58
involved in twelve-step recovery programs	61	39
spend much/most of their free time at the bar	34	66
college professors or academics	65	35
undergraduates	14	86
graduate students	49	51
associated with the University	68	33
associated with the College	30	70
involved with the Lesbian, Gay, and Bisexual Task Force	45	55
involved in political action groups	71	29
active in women's studies	52	48
participate in lesbian support groups	45	55
consider themselves lesbian separatists	8	92
involved in co-counseling	22	78
involved in a long-term relationship with a woman	82	18
lesbian parents	38	62
consider themselves professionals	81	19
currently single	60	40
consider themselves bisexual	18	82
human service professionals	77	23
consider themselves working class	39	61

continued

TABLE 6.1   FRIENDSHIP CHOICES (cont.)

In a Sample of Lesbian and Bisexual Women, 1990 (%, n = 77)

	Many, most, or some of my friends belong to this group	Very few, none, or don't know how many of my friends belong to this group
long-term residents of the City	71	29
women of color	28*	72*
not out as lesbians to many other people	29	71
involved in the arts	49	51

*n = 76

ties, said that the "visible edge of the lesbian community" was some-one who was fifty, fifty-one years old. Although she knew that there was "this whole other world" of house parties, long-term friend-ships, and so forth, she only knew about it from gossip. There were few—if any—links between the feminist and "younger" lesbian community and any groups or social networks of older lesbians.

A Two-Tiered Notion of Community

The difficulty women had in seeing lesbians who were different points to the contradictory notions of community they held. In theory, many held very broad, inclusive definitions of community. Yet when they thought about what lesbian community "looked like" to them, or when they envisioned who belonged in their idea of community, they tended to consider women who looked and acted very much like themselves. This dual notion of community has implications for how lesbian and bisexual women construct boundaries around their social groups—who is allowed in, and who remains excluded.[6]

Deborah Schmidt distinguished between a more and less inclusive vision of community: "I guess when I use it I'm referring to—my initial reaction would be all the lesbians that live in this area; and to some extent that's true. There's a way that I think about it in terms of people that I know. I think when I *say* it, I mean everybody. When I think of what's a picture of it, I think of the lesbians that I know."

Others identified community members in terms of their social participation. For them, lesbian community was defined by those who actively sought out other lesbians. Leslie Mohr argued that, at one level, community was defined by an intentionality, a desire to be recognized as a lesbian and to be involved with others: "I think what I mean is lesbians who want to socialize with other lesbians and want to know other lesbians. So that would include women who play lesbian softball in the summer, women who go to the bar, women who go to the Ferron concerts with their lesbian friends, you know, that kind of thing." But thinking of community more abstractly, Leslie considered, "I guess any lesbian who lives in [the area], in a certain way I would say she's part of the lesbian community in the sense that she's part of the group of lesbians who live here."

Alex Goldman emphasized both self-identification and public visibility: "It's everybody out there who's a lesbian who identifies in some sense with the community and . . . who is publicly affiliated with it in some way." Even though a woman might consider herself a lesbian, if she does not make herself visible at public events or at parties, "then I wouldn't know that they were part of the community."

Because of this two-tiered notion of community, women who are different may experience lesbian community as small, narrow, or exclusive. Bisexual women, women of color, and nonfeminist lesbians, among others, may not find "the" lesbian community the safe haven that white women, women who do not have relationships with men, and feminist lesbians do. In a community based on similarity of lifestyle, on liberal or left politics and "women's music," what happens to Republican lesbians who like opera?

Ilene Zemke aptly described the problem in 1989: "I think it is misleading [to talk about lesbian community]. But it's important. I think it is important for us to feel that we are a part of the community. I think that the problem is that by using that term there are people who feel outside of the community." When women create lesbian community, however broadly, some women are left out.

Margins and Centers: From Both Sides of the Boundaries

If we think of lesbian community as a set of overlapping social circles, it becomes clear that there is no one center—and no single margin—to "the" lesbian community. Some women felt that they were at the margins of several different groups or were not particularly involved with the community at all, while others felt that they were more at "the center." Overall, women seemed less willing to describe themselves as at the center of groups, even when they were described as such by others. A few women did, however, describe themselves as central—or, at least, as *not* marginal. In 1989, Kate Williams described her transition to being a core member of the Lesbian, Gay, and Bisexual Task Force: "I've gotten more involved because there really is a core that runs every group. There's always a core, and I became part of the core because I had the time, first, and I had the energy and the willingness to get involved." By 1994, she was no longer part of the core, in large part because of her feelings of burnout. Although she was still a member of the Task Force, she no longer had a desire to play a public leadership role.

A few women remained part of the core over the five years, but others had pulled back or moved out of town. New women had entered. The core seemed to shift over time.[7]

Commonly, women felt allied with several groups instead of feeling a part of only one group. Wendy Hammond said, "I don't have a group. I mean, I don't identify with the sports group, or the twelve-step group, or the co-counseling group, or whatever groups there are out there. . . . I think there are people in those groups who are exclusively in those groups and don't overlap with others. I don't feel exclusively with any—identified with any group." Wendy had been disappointed by the lack of connections she had made with lesbians as a group. "One of my biggest disappointments in life has been the inability to get people interested in meeting on a regular basis and being supportive of each other as lesbians."

Patrice Amaro fits in with a number of different groups. "I really feel comfortable walking into any kind of political group. I feel comfortable—having played softball and knowing a little bit about it—I enjoy hanging out with women who are involved in softball. I also hav[e] been and am a part of recovery groups; that also feels like safe space. And being at [the University]. Because I have interactions with undergraduate students as well as graduates and everyone else." Although she thinks others would see her as primarily political, she feels comfortable just about everywhere—except among groups who drink heavily or who are not "woman-identified." At the same time, she doesn't see herself as "a group person per se." Rather, she sees her participation as more fluid.

Leslie Mohr sees herself "as a kind of [University] women's studies person, although I also work for the Rape Crisis Center and go to the bar and play softball. But the place in which I'm most visible as a lesbian is definitely at [the University]." Although Leslie was critical of some aspects of lesbian community life, she felt more positive about it than some of her friends, who "felt really burned by it and are suspicious of the desire to have lesbian communities." Leslie felt "more optimistic" about the possibilities of lesbian community life. "I still want to meet lesbians because they are lesbians, you know?"

Softball

Many women connect with other lesbians primarily through soft-ball. In summer, the softball fields are "the" place to see and be seen, a reference point even for those lesbians who don't play. Even women who don't like softball may come down to the fields to hang out with friends, eat hot dogs, and enjoy the atmosphere. There are several teams of varying skill levels that are exclusively lesbian; other teams are mixed. Like other groups in the commu-nity, softball teams have a shifting core. Some groups of women have played together for years. A few women might leave, and oth-ers will join in to take their place. Over the years, teams develop a certain personality and style.

Softball is one of the few places where college and university stu-dents play alongside townies, and class boundaries are somewhat more permeable than elsewhere in the community. But the teams tend to be homogeneous according to age and skill level, and rela-tively few women of color play. Some of the players, like Kim Sny-der, a white woman in her late twenties, are serious athletes who have played competetively and continue to play basketball and other sports in winter. Others are clearly recreational players, involved more for the camaraderie and friendship than for a love of the game.

Kim's team, the Print Shop Players, was going through a period of transition in 1995. A core group of women in their late twenties and thirties had been playing with this team for a number of years, but only in the last year or so had several very competitive, some-what younger members joined. Their team was now one of the strongest in the league, but many of the long-time members were no longer getting playing time. Although all of the women on the team were talented, the coach and some of the players very much wanted to win and a few outstanding athletes received most of the time on the field. Some long-time players unhappily stayed on the bench, game after game. Several players commented on the tension, and before the end of the season, several had left the team. For players like Mariah Cahn, one of the founding members who had left the team, softball games were no longer fun. In a recreational league, Kim commented, it can be "really hard to negotiate" things like "competitiveness and sharing and making sure everyone has fun."

Sue Johnson's team, the Thunderbirds, was older and more clearly recreational. Some of the women on the team had been playing together for ten years. Although a few members were still good ball players, more of the women were in it for fun and companionship—not to win. Playing well, having a good time, being with other women—if they accomplished these things, they felt good about the game. This has been a change for her team: Before, when they were younger, they were "very competitive" and "did very well." Now, they're closer to the bottom of the rankings than the top, but the rankings just don't matter. "It's easy to be sort of nonchalant when you are not winning any games."

An anchor for the community, the softball fields reflect some of the subtle changes in lesbian community life from the late 1980s to the 1990s. By 1994, the lesbian baby boom observed in other cities was well in evidence here. The large number of babies and young children, as well as a few pregnant women—including one pitcher—at the softball fields was striking. Katie Goshen, a woman who had both played and coached for well over a decade, told me that one particular lesbian team had in the last few years had more babies than any other team—lesbian, straight, or mixed. It used to be that many lesbians brought their dogs down to the softball fields. In one year, she said, "All of a sudden it went from a herd of dogs to a herd of babies! It was wonderful." Sue Johnson reiterated the change: "There used to be dozens of dogs, and now there are dozens of kids." Both Katie and Sue remarked that there was much less drinking at the softball fields now. In earlier times, teams would bring coolers full of beer to the games and retire to the bar afterward to celebrate. Now, one of the teams is usually "sober," and very few women, spectators or players, drink alcohol at the fields.

Drawing Back

Not all women watched or played softball, or participated in any of the groups that make up the community. Some felt very distant from the community as a whole and the various groups within it. Cheryl Cook claimed in 1989, for example, that she "was not a joiner." She knew of a number of different groups in town, but she didn't feel especially close to any one group. Although she considered herself a feminist, she felt uncomfortable "with radical lesbian feminists," or with women who "are always looking for somebody to blame for things rather than just take what you have and work with it. Or people who feel that change comes overnight." While she appreciated the informal network of lesbians, which helped her find a supportive lawyer and therapist while she was going through her divorce, she was critical of some of the negative aspects of community life.

Others had been more active in groups at an earlier time in their lives. Anne Biersmith reported: "I've been trying to stay away from being really, really involved. Like, it's been a time of detachment rather than going out and being involved in all kinds of different things. . . . I feel a real pull to *not* be attached for right now."

Several women drew back from participation in the community because of gossip. Before the lesbian and gay bar burned down and reopened on the outskirts of town, Marcela Reyes used to be a "regular" and was very active in other aspects of community life as well. "Everybody knew me, and I knew everybody, when it came to going out and dancing." When she began seeing two women at the same time, she withdrew. "The community is so small here I feel

[word] gets around. . . . I'm very funny about my life getting out on the streets or people knowing who I'm seeing, especially when you're seeing two people."

Wherever they fit in, most of the women spoke about lesbian community life with ambivalence. Even those who had immersed themselves in creating a social, political, and cultural life for lesbians expressed uncertainty. At times the community seemed narrow and exclusive, failing to live up to its ideals of inclusiveness and diversity. After all, no one can force informal friendship networks to expand their boundaries or be more inclusive. And even formal groups may be made to feel more or less hospitable to different women. As Sue Cartledge asked in a 1980 essay, "In a world constructed on friendship, what is the fate of women whom nobody likes very much?"

Some groups are clearly more influential in articulating criteria for inclusion or exclusion—or setting norms and practices for others in the community. In this community, as with some others, feminist and generally leftist political ideals had more currency than other political beliefs. But the importance of feminist goals also extended more broadly. Bonita Brown was puzzled by feminist lesbians' insistence on not shaving their legs, wearing certain kinds of clothing, and eating vegetarian foods. She said, "I never knew that there was a relationship between [lesbianism] and animal rights and being a vegetarian. I never heard about this till I came here." Although she welcomed the opportunity to be with other lesbians, she didn't always feel at home. Like others, she questioned the narrowness and restrictions, but was willing to overlook them because of her desire to connect with other lesbians.

Others have commented on this ambivalence. Arlene Stein notes that at their best lesbian-feminist communities have provided a place for lesbians to proclaim their identities and to nurture and support themselves and other lesbians. By affirming lesbian identities and creating a sense of solidarity, lesbian communities can promote social movement activity and collective action (Buechler 1990; Taylor and Rupp 1993; Taylor and Whittier 1992). Yet in so doing, women who don't fit in are left out. Many women struggled with this tension. While wanting to reject the exclusivity inherent in a community of friendship networks, they clung to an ideal of lesbian community as a place of acceptance and a celebration of lesbian life, lesbian sexuality, and lesbian politics.

7
Rule Making and Rule Breaking

"Whichever group it is that you're talking about, be it the jocks, the academics, the politicos, the whatever—I see each group as having a kind of standard. Almost like . . . membership rules. You know, these are the rules that you have to meet in order to be a member of our group. . . . And they're crazy things, like what kind of clothes you wear, how short your haircut is, who your other friends are. . . . I mean, each little group has its own particular rules." Alex Goldman was explicit about the rule making she saw in the lesbian community. "In my own case, and this is purely personal, I feel like the groups that I was interested in breaking into were very difficult to break into because I was not a part of a couple." Alex described in some detail instances of others who had been accepted by the social circles she had wanted to gain entry to. "I kind of felt judged by them . . . you know, maybe for the way I dressed."

Louise Pratt said that it wasn't only lesbian communities that had rules, but other groups as well. In 1989, she said, "We see that certainly not only in the political or lesbian community. . . . You know, if you're a born-again Christian, [the rule is] 'only born-again Christians are gonna go to heaven and everybody else is gonna go to hell.'" For herself, however, Louise didn't pay much attention to rule breaking. "I don't care much about what people think or say about me." At the same time, she said, "I'm such a good girl; it's very hard for me to relate to this concept of breaking rules."

Joan Borman didn't feel that she had ever broken any kind of spoken or unspoken rule, but she did sometimes feel "out of synch" with others in the community. In 1989, before a life crisis sparked a major reassessment, she said, "I think that I'm often viewed as someone who takes life too seriously and just can't be more relaxed about things. So that makes me feel a bit out of synch. But I've never, never had the feeling that I've violated some sacred rule. . . . I guess I feel like there have been times when I felt as if the prevailing norm in the community—again, a lot depends on who one is assuming is the community, right? But that the prevailing norm in the community, for example, has been a much more, 'I'm alright—you're alright' kind of mode than I would feel comfortable with."

Joan also likes to dress up, but finds little support for that here. "There are relatively few women who go places here and take it as an opportunity for maybe wearing make-up. Putting on dressy clothes." By 1994, Joan felt a lot freer to dress as she pleased. She recalled a time "when I thought I had to wear work boots and give up any kind of dressing up, because I was in a lesbian-feminist community and it just didn't do that. Period." Her feelings of greater freedom were probably due as much to changes in her attitude as they were to changes in the community. But Susan Becker, too, felt in 1994 that fems like herself were much more accepted than even five years earlier. "Women are more comfortable being feminine. I think more lesbians are being comfortable with that side of them."

Setting Standards

Where do norms come from? What kind of feedback tells women if they're in step or out of synch? Some, like Ilene Zemke and Laurel Jameson, read national lesbian and feminist publications like *Off Our Backs, Lesbian Connection,* and *Sojourner.* "A lot is debated in the women's and lesbian press. Many people don't read these papers, and they're lucky," said Ilene. "But I read them all and get very angry. And the letters columns, I always turn to the letters column first, so I see what is the national debate, and that often dictates what the local debate will be."

Laurel has become suspicious of lesbian writing. As a bisexual, she constantly feels out of step. "There have been some mighty good women around here who have been very accepting, and we have a good time with that. But reading lesbian writing makes me aware. . . . Every time I read that damn paper I know that I failed again." Laurel talked about reading a popular lesbian book: "I was aware that I was really, really, explosively politically incorrect and subversive and everything else that was wrong. So it's not just [this] community. It's also when I pick up some reading and find out what other people are doing around the country, then I realize in certain ways I'm really out of it."

Some have felt out of step based on the personal reactions of others. Leslie Mohr, for example, recounted being told that she doesn't "look like" a lesbian. "The whole issue of not looking like a lesbian is about that. It's that kind of judgment. . . . I feel like there's the embedded accusation that I'm trying to pass, that I'm trying to pass as straight and get some privilege there. . . . There was one particular woman who just a couple of times said that to me. You know, 'You don't look like a lesbian,' in a kind of accusing way. And then somebody else said it to me after I had talked to her about it, and I said, 'God, this is so stupid. I *am* a lesbian. This is what a lesbian looks like, you know?' . . . It was really kind of reinforcing that notion that there is a way to look, and you don't measure up."

Patrice Amaro sometimes felt she could never live up to others' expectations. "If I don't do enough lesbian stuff, then I'm not behind the politics. I'm not there like I'm supposed to be. I can't get real specific with it, because it's just a feeling I get, and it's a comment that is thrown at me by young women. . . . Or I get shunned. I mean, that's happened, too. . . . I don't like walking around in a community when I've had close contact with people and not being spoken to. I mean, that's just weird stuff."

Alex Goldman described a similar phenomenon her first few years in the city: not being invited to dinners or parties. Although people were nice to her when they met her downtown or at events, she rarely was invited to women's homes.

Several people described physical reactions—drawing back, or making faces. Alex caught herself doing this. A woman she knew was dating a woman who was involved with somebody else. "She was talking quite openly about that she was involved with one of them. These two other women had primary relationships, she'd gotten involved." When Alex found out who the other women were, she made a face and said, "Aah . . . that explains!" And then she caught herself: "You know, I really need to retract that facial expression and that grunt. . . . I have absolutely no basis for judging either of them." Even though she had felt criticized by others, she found herself doing the same.

Susan Becker also recalled a physical response to her fem clothing and make-up. At a party, she felt that several lesbians assumed she was heterosexual and judged her harshly. "I saw *immediately,* I mean it was almost a physical drawing back . . . I got an immediate, instinctive feeling that these women would not be able to accept talking to me about, like a good trashy mystery, or you know, my toenail polish or something. There's almost a physical withdrawing. . . . I've encountered it many times."

Ilene Zemke argued that this kind of rule making emerges from lesbians' outsider status. "Nobody wants to be an outsider, so we work very hard to make certain rules that will make us insiders within that grouping. But the lessons we've learned about how to analyze culture or politics are learned from the world at large, from the patriarchal, male-dominated world." She sees the attempt to set rigid rules for behavior as terribly destructive to the community, and—despite the negative connotations—thinks of herself as a libertarian, "dirty word though that may be." Ilene tempered that by saying, "I'm intolerant in my private life, I'm quick to anger, and I'm quick to feel intolerant. But in the larger scheme, and politically and socially, I try very hard to cultivate extreme tolerance. I think anything less than that is fascist, and that lesbianism and lesbians in this country right now have a tendency that is leaning much more to the right than to the left, and much more toward fascism than anything else, when we exclude and when we label with harshness and disparaging terms." Ilene worried about this trend: "It is something that really haunts me."

Normative Accounts

Even the most rebellious and uppity dykes create patterned ways of living. Through formal and informal processes, individuals in all social groups learn what behaviors, beliefs, and skills are valued for people like themselves, and how to conform to, rebel against, or at least be aware of the expectations of the group. Family members teach how to be a well-behaved "Esterberg" or "Smith" or "Garcia"; church or synagogue members teach how to be an observant Unitarian or Jew; African Americans teach how to survive in a white-dominated community; and so on. At the same time, simply holding valued identities may increase the likelihood of behaving according to the expectations of the group (Stryker 1980; Smith-Lovin and Heise 1988). People *care* about their identities, and they act in ways that confirm their senses of who they are.

Yet lesbian and bisexual women typically do not learn in childhood or early adolescence how to be "good" lesbians or bisexuals. From a very early age, most women are channeled toward heterosexuality, encouraged to date and make themselves attractive to men, and expected to focus their ambitions on marriage and motherhood (see Rich [1980] for an extended discussion of compulsory heterosexuality). With very few exceptions, most social institutions and heterosexual parents do not pass along much information about lesbian, gay, and bisexual life. When information does pass through, it is often distorted and biased. Contacts with lesbian communities may be one of the first—and most important—ways in which lesbian and bisexual women learn which norms and behaviors are valued and which are not.

Not all members of a group behave exactly in accordance with the stated and unstated rules for behavior. Individuals may have greater or lesser awareness of norms, based on how long they have participated in the community, what cliques and social groups they have been involved in, and how sensitive they are to social rules. Some people are more conforming, while others delight in flouting convention. Politically active lesbians may be especially rebellious and critical of social rules. Sarah Lucia Hoagland contends, for example, that "refusal to conform is part of what makes us lesbians" (1988, p. 11).

Unearthing accounts of norms through surveys and interviews is difficult. Social rules arise in interaction, over time; they are situational and subject to change. In one sense, norms are not "real"; they are hard to pin down because they are rarely stated so baldly. Few in the community would argue outright, for example, that lesbians *should* look androgynous, or wear short hair, slacks, and Birkenstock sandals. More than one woman who looked like this argued that she didn't care about rules for behavior.[1] But conforming to rules, regardless of one's intentions, typically passes un-noticed. It is mostly in breaking social rules that they become apparent. Too, verbal accounts cannot capture the facial expressions, double entendres, and gestures that indicate a social gaffe. Nor can they capture the feeling in the pit of one's stomach or the flushed cheek that might indicate a social embarrassment.

Despite this difficulty, three general normative accounts were found in the community. Like identity accounts, normative accounts reveal individuals' stories about the formal and informal rules for behavior they believe exist in the community. Each of the three accounts documents a cluster of interrelated norms. The first account centers around political beliefs and values; the second focuses on egalitarian values; and the third centers around libertarian ideals and resistance to conformity.

POLITICS: Women who endorsed the first account, which centers around political values and behaviors, are strongly committed to social change. They strongly agreed that "it's important to be radical about lifting oppression from every aspect of life" and that "lesbianism is connected to other issues, like racism, sexism, and oppression of other groups." They also felt that it's "important to live your life according to your political ideals."

Joan Borman exemplifies some of the tensions involved in living according to a set of political ideals without judging others or being inflexible. "I think that there are certain issues, situations that require serious, serious acts of moral responsibility. . . . In some ways I think that as I get older I become less doctrinaire, but more committed to the things that I really believe in. I mean, I'm willing to be flexible, in more areas, and just say, 'Well, I don't know. That's sort of an interesting perspective. I've never really thought about that.' At the same time, you know, being absolutely unequivocal about things that I think are really horrendous, like apartheid in South Africa."

Joan believes strongly that she must take responsibility for her political beliefs. "I don't think that I'm less fervent now than I was, in fact probably more fervent about it, insisting people have real responsibilities for their actions." Although there are times when it would be easier to "take the line of least resistance," she feels a commitment to respond. For example, when "I am an unwitting observer to some unpleasant interaction that is clearly defined as racist. But I'm not a party to it, except that I feel like I have a responsibility to be a party to it. So maybe I open my mouth and I say something, or find a way to intervene. Now I don't call that political correctness. I say, well, I'm a white person in this society, and I have to be responsible for those privileges. I have to. It's not a question of feeling guilty that I have them. It is [a question of] what do I do with the fact that I have them? How do I use them in some kind of appropriate way, so that I can do my part in alleviating what is clearly an offensive and oppressive situation for people of color."

Women like Joan clearly reject separatism. They agree that gay men and lesbians should work together, although they are somewhat less affirming that lesbians and gay men have much in common.

Susan Becker has increasingly become active in statewide gay and lesbian politics. As she sees it, gender "should be a nonissue" in this kind of organizing. Given the threats posed by the religious right, men and women have got to work together. Still, her world is composed primarily of women, and she sees herself as an active feminist. Especially during times when she is not actively involved in a political organization, she feels it is important "to live my life in a way to illustrate feminist ideals."

Interestingly, a number of women believed that working with men or having close friendships with men would be negatively sanctioned by the community. For example, Kate Williams mentioned that several of her friends did not want to work with the Lesbian, Gay, and Bisexual Task Force because men were involved in that group. And Alex Goldman talked about not wanting to have a working dinner at a restaurant with a male colleague, fearing community gossip. Yet none of the three normative accounts, including this first one, affirmed separatism as a value.

A strong norm for this group was being open about one's sexual orientation. Susan Becker, for example, changed enormously from 1989 to 1994. At the earlier time, she was mostly closeted—especially at work. By 1994, in contrast, she saw herself as almost completely open—a "10" on a scale from 1 to 10.

Denny Slater was glad that some women were able to be out all the time. "I think that there are women who believe that it's very important to let everyone know that they're a lesbian. And to wear their pink triangles, to have their short cropped hair, to have buttons or visible means of [saying] 'I am a lesbian and I'm in your face.' And I think that they feel that women who do not put it out there are compromising our movement. And God bless them, in a certain kind of way, you know. I'm glad people have the ability to take that extreme."

Others, too, mentioned that they felt being out was an important norm in the community. The only time Deborah Schmidt felt she had broken an unspoken community rule was when she couldn't be totally out at work. "There are times when I have even lied about that [being a lesbian], which felt uncomfortable."

Feminist values are important to this account. For Deborah, feminism means "bringing my experience of life as a woman" to "whatever issue I'm involved in." Feminism isn't disconnected from her other political engagements. "I think I bring a different perspective to all sorts of issues because I am a woman, and because I have thought about what it means to me to be a woman in this society."

Deborah admires committed living: "I know a lot of people who have made political—not political, necessarily—but have made decisions not to do certain things and to try to live their lives in a certain way because of their beliefs. . . . It's living it out, not talking about it necessarily or judging people who are not living that same way. That's great. That's inspiring to me."

EGALITARIAN VALUES: Women who identified with the second account, which centers on egalitarian values, resolutely affirmed equality in their relationships, and they held strong beliefs about how lesbians should be treated—and how they should treat each other. Egalitarian values, both within their relationships and within the larger heterosexist society, were paramount.

Ilene Zemke felt that lesbian relationships were more likely to be equal than heterosexual ones. "I think there's more room for striving for balance of power among women than there might be between a man and a woman. I think that is very important in a relationship." At the same time, she criticized harshly what she described as "mental sadomasochism" within relationships, by which she means "keeping somebody on their toes and insecure in a relationship. One person having more economic power than another, and not owning it, not admitting it, not trying to work out ways for equanimity [*sic*]." Irene says that she sees it "a lot, more than I'm comfortable with, and it makes me really cringe. It makes me uncomfortable, and I think it's more painful and more hurtful than anything else."

Alex Goldman articulated some of the ironies of being a strong woman in a lesbian relationship. "I'm a pretty strong—dominating—person. In a lesbian relationship, I got shit on for that. You know, 'cause you're not supposed to dominate." You should "strive towards egalitarian everything, and it's *bad* for one woman to dominate another. But I almost feel a little bit more freedom to be dominating—forceful—in a heterosexual relationship, and I get feminist rhetorical support for that. Because to do opposite would be to be subordinated."

This group stressed the value of long-term relationships. At the same time, they did not approve of butch-fem relationships, unlike others who see in them a distinctive lesbian history and culture (e.g., Kennedy and Davis 1993; Nestle 1992).

Kate Williams, who had come out as a lesbian in the South at a time in which butch-fem roles were common, is one of those who were critical: "I haven't been in a role since I first came out. I don't like male and female roles. They don't work for heterosexuals, and I don't think they work for homosexuals. So butch-fem isn't for me."

She described when she first came out: "I was considered fem automatically. First of all, I was very young. Long hair . . . I consider myself androgynous now, but [I was] very feminine for that era. And I had no experience, you know, and so I had no choice. As far as I was concerned, call me fem all you want, 'cause you're right, 'cause I don't have any experience. And then about [my] third or fourth lover, I started identifying myself as sort of butch. And it's because I was getting involved with women who were younger, and who didn't have very much experience, and I had more than they did—which was not a lot. And then I finally got sick of that role, because I ended up living with a lover who was very role-oriented and really abused the role. So, and then I went, I don't want to do this. . . . I don't want to copy the straight world. It's not working in the straight world, so why would I want to copy it in my own life?"

Women in this group supported, though only moderately, commitment ceremonies as a way to affirm long-term relationships. Although in this city lesbian and gay couples can register as domestic partners at city hall, very few of the women had actually done so. Kate was one of the few. Being in a domestic partnership, however, does not mean that her relationship is patterned on a traditional heterosexual model. She and her partner have bought a home together, but they each have separate rooms and a great deal of autonomy.

In this second normative account, as with the first, politics are important. Women agreed strongly that "it's important to live your life according to your political ideals."

Ilene sometimes feels as though she's "living in an occupied camp." As a feminist, she thinks, "you're under siege" because feminism has been so discredited in recent years. Yet she sees feminism "as an impulse to do good in the world that would make women be empowered. . . . And the more we are empowered, truly empowered and imbued with kindness, we will make a good world." As she goes about her daily business, she earnestly tries to live up to these ideals. "I am one of the people who believes that you start with yourself. Make yourself whole, so that you're not carrying around garbage. And baggage. Then step out of yourself. Get over yourself so that you can reach out to someone else."

This account also stressed the importance of women's rights and the need to be vigorous in changing attitudes about lesbians. Women who endorsed this account emphasized commonalities among lesbians, adding that they felt lesbians are much freer than heterosexual women and that lesbians should commit themselves to working with other lesbians.

One of the things Wendy Hammond likes most about being a lesbian is the bond she shares with other lesbians. "It's very important to me. My friends, my community of gay people. There's something really a lot of fun to me about all being in the same boat together, that I really enjoy. There's the commonality, the bond from that. The surviving: women surviving in spite of the non-supportive attitudes of society. . . . The humor that we seem to share in our oppression is very important to me. I can't imagine what it must be like to be a heterosexual woman. I mean, there's something wonderful about the special identity I have for being lesbian. It feels like a very, very special group of people to be associated with."

LIBERTARIAN IDEALS: If the first account is defined by its political stance and the second by the importance of egalitarian values, then the third account is defined by its outright rejection of rigid norms and prescriptions for behavior. The women endorsing this account rejected the notion that there was any single way that lesbians ought to behave—especially in terms of dress and appearance and social relationships with men.

Cheryl Cook, for example, prides herself on her independent thinking. When first asked about norms and prescriptions for behavior, she shook her head. "I define it as group think. As, you should identify with this group, and they tell you politically how you should feel on certain issues. . . . To me, it's another form of religion, you know. And somebody will tell *me* how to think!"

Kate Foster described political correctness: "It's acceptance of the paradigm and . . . from that certain prescriptions for behavior will follow. . . . It's also very status oriented." Kate rejected the notion that there is one way to behave: "I'm not willing to live with those kinds of boundaries in terms of my own behaviors, how I present myself to the world, or the people I choose to be emotionally close to."

Bonita Brown doesn't like being part of social groups. When the softball team she was part of needed to raise funds, she did not want to participate because she didn't feel she could ask people for money. "I'm not very good at social groups like that. I like playing softball, . . . but I felt like I was being coerced into, you know, well if you don't do this you're not 'really' a lesbian. . . . And I just felt, that's why I don't join groups, because I don't want to have to do—if I do fifteen out of sixteen things they do, I don't want to do the sixteenth one just because I'm part of the group."

Women who endorsed this account felt strongly that lesbians should not be judgmental about each other. Deb Smith felt that at an earlier point in her life she had been very intolerant of others: "I can remember when I was pretty hard-nosed about somebody being lesbian. . . . And I was pretty obnoxious. Now I think maybe it had more to do with me being uncomfortable. . . . Well, one, that I was just getting in touch with my own lesbianism and women's culture, and so it may have something more to do with not feeling secure with myself." Now, she hopes she is more open-minded.

Judy Clausner, too, recalled a time during the 1970s when she was much more judgmental and had kicked a roommate out of her apartment for becoming involved with a man. Years later, when she herself became involved with a man, she understood but was still angered and hurt by the criticism she received.

This normative account emphasized freedom of choice. Women in this group reacted negatively to the notion that lesbians should not socialize with men or dress in traditionally feminine ways. They felt it was important to be able to reconsider their lesbianism after they came out, and they felt they should be able to challenge other lesbians who are judgmental.

Patrice Amaro told several stories about being "put in her place" for criticizing other lesbians. In one instance, when she was living in another city in the same state, she felt that some of the women were poorly treating male police officers who were assigned to a Take Back the Night march. "They did not see that their violence was just as ugly as the violence that has been demonstrated by our culture. And so when I brought that up, I was put in my place very quickly."

Both Sally Zimmerman and Judy Clausner were heavily criticized when they began relationships with men after identifying themselves as lesbians. Although Sally's close friends were supportive, others were not. "People didn't quite know what to make of it. Some people were pleased; other people were outraged." Three years after she married the man she was involved with, some people still were not talking to her. Judy's experience was similar: "For my good friends, it wasn't a problem." But for others, it was more difficult.

Although women in this group felt strongly about norms and prescriptions for behavior, they also felt strongly about equality within relationships. As with the other two groups, they were strong advocates for women's equality, and felt that people should live according to their political ideals.

Deb Smith sees feminism as entailing equality between men and women; it also involves bringing about "a balance of male/ female principles in this culture" and giving "all human beings the opportunity to develop in whatever wonderful way they can." For Deb, feminism has been an important part of her creative work since the early 1970s. As a teacher, she says, "I was very opinion- ated and more or less wanting people to see my point of view. . . . I wanted students to recognize the injustices, and to really take se- riously the oppression of women." Although she hopes she is now a little less "hard-nosed" in her approach, she still takes her femi- nism very seriously.

More succinctly, Cheryl Cook said, "I'm a female advocate. I see the world through a woman's eyes, and I always will. I believe in women."

Passing Judgment and Political Correctness

That lesbian communities can be judgmental and restrictive may not be surprising given the hostility of the larger society in which they are embedded. But the issue of judgmentalness itself came under scrutiny during the 1980s, as women debated the issue of "political correctness." At the time, many saw the issue as an un- critical acceptance of certain political beliefs, values, and behav- iors, and a judgmentalness toward those who disagreed. For a while, it seemed, it even became fashionable to claim political *in*- correctness. Many joked about it, and some sported buttons read- ing "politically incorrect."

But by the early 1990s, the issue of political correctness was no longer an in-joke or internal debate, but more an issue of language. For at least some women, the increasingly conservative political climate served as a wake-up call. As right wing commentators, politicians, and others attacked the principles of inclusion, feminism, and multiculturalism embodied in "political correctness," the ardor with which these debates had been conducted in the lesbian community was dampened. By then, many feminists and lesbians, like Ilene Zemke, felt under siege.

Commentators have made much of the tendency toward conformity in feminist lesbian communities (see, e.g., Barnhart 1975; Krieger 1983; Faderman 1991, pp. 230–45).[2] Some have explained the tendency toward conformity and building boundaries as arising from the loss of self that arises in a community based on likeness.[3] For example, Susan Krieger (1983) argues that lesbian community provides a basic "identity conflict" to participants. While the community provides the potential for validation of lesbian identities, women's uniqueness and individuality are not valued. Some women may experience themselves as either subordinated to or abandoned by the community. Alex Goldman's feelings of hurt and anger at the community's seeming lack of interest in her are suggestive.

Others have argued that the tendency toward conformity is an outgrowth of identity politics (A. Stein 1992; Weston 1991). In a community and movement based on sameness of identity, differences are not easily tolerated.[4] Those who are different are seen as unstable allies, not to be counted on.

Still other commentators see conformity as part of *all* social movements. This kind of rule making emerges, Muriel Dimen argues, when individuals attempt "to bring the unsatisfactory present in line with the utopian future" (1984, pp. 138–39). Anne Biersmith offered this sentiment: Reflecting on the difficulty in living according to a set of political ideals, she said, "I don't think people should get so judgmental. . . . But everybody's just trying to push each other in the right direction, I suppose. I think we want each other to be better people."

8

Bisexual Accounts and the Limits of Lesbian Community

For Laurel Jameson, acknowledging her feelings about women was a revelation: "Oh, to be able to love women and relate to women without that awful barrier. And to acknowledge that dumpy, middle-aged women are so beautiful to me. I like them a little on the older side, a little on the tubby side, I think. And to allow that delicious, physical, beautiful feeling to be there." But Laurel sees herself as "sitting in the middle." "What I'm looking for is to allow this man to be there, but not in a way that cripples and damages and puts barriers up."

If relationships with straight women are sometimes difficult, so are relations with lesbians. "You see, if I have to be in the closet around straight people because they don't like that I like girls, so in the same way I've got to be kind of in the closet around lesbians because they're really quite put off by this man. . . . I can get shot down from both sides. It's a weird sensation."

Although lesbians and bisexuals have coexisted for years, bisexuality has just been discovered by the popular media. As *Newsweek* proclaimed in the July 1995 cover article, bisexuality is in, chic, and almost new, the "wild card of our erotic life," just now "coming out in the open—in pop culture, in cyberspace, and on campus."

For the bisexual women who have long worked within lesbian communities, there is little new, chic, or popular about their situation. Bisexuals have pressed for recognition within lesbian communities, with mixed success; in some larger coastal cities, they have worked toward creating an autonomous bi movement and community. Although in a few places lesbians and bisexuals have worked peaceably together, tensions have been longstanding. Bisexual women have been called fence sitters, traitors, and spreaders of disease. Lesbians who have found themselves in the uneasy situation of falling in love with men have faced the loss of community.

The mass media's depiction of bisexuals as chic threesomes and trendy urban swingers is only one possible formulation of bisexual identity.[1] Like lesbian identities, bisexual identities are not homogeneous. Some come unwillingly to a bisexual identity after years of identifying as lesbian. Others come to think of themselves as bisexual during a first love affair with a woman. Still others develop a bisexual identity hypothetically, based on unacted-upon sexual attractions.

"Not Quite Heterosexual"

Helen Bradfield, a young white woman who is just finishing graduate school, calls herself "not quite heterosexual." In 1994, she was living with a man, the same man she had been involved with since her undergraduate years; they were married a year after the interview. Helen has never been romantically or sexually involved with a woman. She felt attracted to both men and women when she first became involved with E., her partner, but she did not act on it. Increasingly, Helen sees her bisexuality as an intellectual proposition, a potentiality that will probably not be realized rather than an active part of her life. It is more a "willingness to consider the possibility that I might become romantically involved or interested in other women." Sometimes she thinks it's "sort of silly" to think of herself as bisexual because the chances that she will actually enter into a relationship with a woman are relatively small.

Because of her monogamous relationship, she tends not to talk to others about her bisexuality. Although "it is important to me that it not be something that *I* just know," it feels odd to come out to people as a bisexual. "It would be more artificial to do that, I think, than let people think I'm heterosexual." To some extent, she says, "I frequently feel like a fraud in a lot of different ways because I certainly consider this [having a relationship with a woman] to be a possibility, but I am sure that most of the people who know me don't." At the same time, she says, "I also worry that I am being a fraud in the sense that I am letting people make that assumption [that she is heterosexual] and in particular letting E. not have to think about it." He knows that she has been attracted to women, but she has not talked about it with him recently.

Helen may be quiet about her own sexuality, but she is not quiet about her support for lesbians and gays. One of her concerns about being more open about her feelings for women is that she feels she might be a more effective supporter if she is perceived as heterosexual. "I wonder sometimes whether the most useful position for me to be in, as someone who supports gays and lesbians, is to act as someone who is not in that group, but supports them. And I wonder if that's a more persuasive model for other heterosexuals." Although she has both lesbian and bisexual friends and has been to some events, she is not active in the lesbian community. She does not want to make lesbians uncomfortable because of her relationship with E. "I don't want people to see me as an intruder."

Chrissy Herek's identity account is similar in that she talks about her identity tentatively. Like Helen, she is very private about her sexuality. For Chrissy, being bisexual means being "flexible," open to both men and women. She says, "It was very hard for me to realize that there wasn't a black and white in my situation." While she was fairly comfortable saying to herself that she is bisexual, she was not comfortable telling others and was still "exploring how other people will feel." In some contexts, depending on who she is talking to, she might say "I consider myself heterosexual, but I'm open."

At the time of the interview, Chrissy was in her first relationship with a woman, a friend she had met in school. Neither of the two had ever been involved with a woman before, and the relationship grew out of their close friendship. Although Chrissy had felt attracted to women in high school, she resisted those feelings. "At one point, I did feel like I didn't know which way I was gonna go. So I just forced myself to be with men all the time." At the same time, she said, "I knew I wasn't being true to other feelings I was having." She dated men throughout high school and through much of her time in college. Just about the same time that she realized "I don't have to look just there in men," she began to develop romantic feelings for her best friend. Several months before the interview, Chrissy and G. became lovers.

Unlike Helen, Chrissy knows very few bisexuals or lesbians. When she first began to think she might be attracted to G., she sought help and support from a teacher, one of the few open lesbians or bisexuals she knew. She also knows a classmate who is struggling with her sexual identity and might be bisexual. While she would like more support, she fears what she calls "straight" lesbians, whom she sees as "cold and hard, defensive." She doesn't want to "fall into a stereotype," but she says she feels good about being "open" to both men and women. "Sexual identity, for me, I feel is and always will be a growing experience. If the door is open, and if you allow yourself—if you have the time and the energy to share with somebody, continually, and to let it grow, anything could happen."

For both Helen and Chrissy, bisexuality involves a kind of openness and flexibility. Yet their bisexuality is emphatically not experienced socially, within the context of a social group or community.

For Helen, it is constructed mainly in her mind; for Chrissy, it is constructed within the cocoon of her relationship with G. Other people tend to see them as heterosexual, an impression they tend not to challenge even as it makes them uncomfortable.

Their accounts are defined by a certain tentativeness about claiming a bisexual identity. Still, being "not quite heterosexual" is not necessarily a bridge to another identity—either lesbian or heterosexual. Helen's identity seems fairly stable: she is married and has been in a committed relationship for a long time now. In contrast, Chrissy's seems more changeable. Because her relationship with G. and her thinking of herself as "open" was so new at the time of the interview, it is likely that over time she may think of herself somewhat differently.[2] For some, then, an identity as "not quite heterosexual" may be transitional; for others, like Helen, this identity account may be more enduring.

Open Bisexuality

Pat Lawler and Laurel Jameson are both in their early to mid fifties. They have been married to men (two marriages each), and both came to think of themselves as bisexual somewhat later in life, when they were in their late thirties and forties. Both are mothers of adult children who no longer live at home. They live alone, a situation neither wishes to change at the moment. Although their styles of presentation are very different—Laurel is flamboyant, and Pat is very quiet—their accounts of their bisexuality are strikingly similar. Both tend to eschew labels, but—in the context of an interview, at least—think of themselves as bisexuals. They tend to be open about their sexuality, their friends are primarily lesbians, and they participate in lesbian events. Both Pat and Laurel are sometimes thought of as lesbians by others, a perception they typically don't care to correct. Pat sometimes thinks of herself as a lesbian, depending on the context. Both consider themselves feminists.

Laurel Jameson was leaving an abusive marriage when she first began to see herself as bisexual. At the time, she entered into a battered women's support group and was encouraged to explore her feelings of attraction for women. Although she said she first wanted to "transmogrify into a lesbian," she knew that a lesbian identity did not incorporate all of who she was. At the time, she said, "I feel like I'm in-between. I'm definitely lesbian-identified, yet I also include men in my life." When first interviewed in 1989, Laurel saw her bisexuality as intertwined with her growing sense of independence. She said, "I'm woman-identified, I am self-identified, and being more and more self-led. I'm acknowledging that I find women attractive and that that's been the case, but always shoved off to the periphery. But I'm also willing to love certain men, if they're willing to be honest and decent about their homophobia, and about their sexism."

For Laurel, bisexuality entails an expansiveness. It means that she can have breakfast with her lesbian friends each week at a local diner, "when it's lesbian time," when they take over the tables. She can dance at the local gay bar, flirt with women at the food cooperative, and still relate to men if she chooses. At the time of the first interview, Laurel was actively involved in the Lesbian and Gay Task Force, and she was instrumental in changing the name to include bisexuals. Then, she felt it was important to "claim the word 'bisexual' and not have to apologize for it, or shuffle around, or look stupid." She saw herself as "rather boldly out." "You see, I've got this wonderful bisexual pride left, and I wear my pink triangle. And I realize that maybe that's, at this point, maybe the best thing I can do for us—bi's, gays, alike—and that is to be visible, to make myself visible and take the risk."

At the time of the second interview, Laurel's situation had not changed much. She said, "I still feel queer as a three-dollar bill. That has not changed." But she has entered back into a relationship with her former husband, who is seriously ill, but who does not live with her. She said, "A lesbian would not want a man in her life in this way. And so . . . I'm bi. And bi people do this. Bi people do this. And it doesn't mean that we're any less identified with the gay community. Any less committed to gay rights, gay lifestyle. Any less loving the [gay bar] and the coffeehouse. Any less wanting to work for the gay community. It means that we're more than just—it means we have a wider range of responses. I have a wider range of responses."

Although Laurel identifies herself with the lesbian community and doesn't mind being thought of as lesbian, she feels it's more honest and accurate to present herself as bisexual. Sometimes she thinks of herself as queer. "I don't know that I can properly say lesbian. If lesbian includes—it depends on how you define it. I'm a lesbian if bisexuality is included. And I'm not afraid of the 'l-word.' I mean, I'll walk around with a big sign. . . . I don't mind that a bit. I feel bi is more honest, because if I walk in and say I'm a lesbian, and then later on you see me walking down the street with this sick old man, you'll wonder what happened. And I'd rather be honest. So I don't surprise anybody."

At the same time, she doesn't want to be constrained by labels. Although she feels there's a time and a place when labels are important, she would like bisexuality to continue to be expansive. "I hope we don't get a politically correct way to be bisexual. 'You have to do this. To be bisexual you have to have a man in your closet.' I hope there isn't something we have to *do* to *be*. And the way bisexuality was, it wasn't that I had to read the right books and have the right haircut and quote Mary Daly and wear a labyris and do all these things. It was precisely that there were no standards. . . . I hope that doesn't happen, but I don't know."

Like Laurel, Pat Lawler has a clear sense of herself as bisexual. Yet she also dislikes labels and says, "If you weren't interviewing me I would not put myself in that category. I usually don't label myself." When asked, however, she says, "I pretty much identify myself as bisexual. I have had relationships with both men and women since the end of my second marriage. I've been married twice. I have friendships with people of both sexes. I enjoy the company of both men and women, but my closest, closest friendships are with women who identify themselves as either lesbians or bisexuals." Sometimes, depending on the context, she thinks of herself as lesbian. "I think it has almost more to do with the setting than with anything going on inside of me. When I'm with a group of lesbians or lesbian and bisexual women, it's like I generally relate to women."

Pat doesn't usually talk explicitly about her sexuality. She is known throughout her workplace because of her union activities. "I think most people regard me as a lesbian. Not because I've ever said it. Not because I've made it an issue. But because I've done things, . . . like sponsor a gay-lesbian-bisexual group. Because of political positions I've taken. People have made that assumption. And I don't say anything to dissuade them or persuade them one way or another. It's just who I am and they can deal with me in whatever way they think."

Although she has had satisfying sexual relationships with men since she's come out, Pat has not had what she calls satisfying "total relationships, what I consider a relationship that's loving and mutually supportive." Like Laurel, she chafes at the traditional gender roles of heterosexual relationships. "It's a struggle with relationships with men not to fall into very traditional kinds of roles. The male as protector, the provider sort of thing; the female, the caretaker and homemaker sort of thing." Relationships with women are much easier in that regard, but for a variety of reasons she sees herself as staying single for the foreseeable future.

For both Laurel and Pat, sexual identity issues are not of foremost importance right now. Far more important are nurturing friendships, taking care of their health, and generally taking what comes from day to day. Laurel is currently taking a rest from political activism. Although both would like greater acceptance of bisexuals within the lesbian community—and the heterosexual community, Pat adds—they feel that the community is more open than it has been in the past. Building a separate, autonomous bisexual community is not presently on the agenda for either of these women.

Formerly Lesbian Bisexuals

Other women come to a bisexual identity after a strong identification as lesbian. For these women, finding themselves attracted to men after immersion in the lesbian community was a struggle. Sally Zimmerman, whose story is discussed in Chapter 3, found herself in this position, as did Alex Goldman. Both became outsiders in the community that they had so actively participated in earlier.

Judy Clausner, a Jewish woman in her early fifties, had a similar experience. She came to this community over twelve years ago. Before then, she had lived in a major city with a large, politically active lesbian community. In many respects, Judy's early experiences parallel Joan Borman's, which were discussed in earlier chapters. Judy was actively involved in the feminist movement when she came out as a lesbian. Like Joan, she says that she was a feminist first, then a lesbian. "Frankly, I don't think I would have come out if it wasn't for the women's movement. I'm really someone who came out as a feminist first, and then I became a lesbian." At the time, in the 1970s, she identified "very heavily" as a lesbian. She was part of a semi-professional, politically active segment of the lesbian community. In the large city she used to live in: "I was very out. I was out because of the work I was doing. I was sort of well-known, so I was very out. And it was important to me to live my politics."

In the 1980s, however, Judy's experience diverged sharply from Joan's. Although she doesn't actively call herself bisexual, she doesn't think of herself as straight either. She does not typically think of herself as having a sexual identity. "I'm attracted to both men and women," she said. "And that's just where it's at, period."

For most of the 1970s, Judy was in monogamous relationships with women. When she moved to this community, she came to be with a woman lover. After that relationship broke up in the mid 1980s, she decided to reconsider her feelings for men. Judy had always found the norms and rules of the lesbian community annoying. By this time, she found the community far too restricting. She said, "Nobody's telling me what to do. I'm really my own person. I can do whatever I want. I don't have to go out with women; I don't have to just go out with men. . . . I thought, wait a second, I can go out with whomever I [am] attracted to."

When she first began relating to men, however, she did care about what others thought of her. Because she had been so active and open, withdrawing from the lesbian community was difficult. Like Sally Zimmerman, she found that people stopped inviting her to events that she used to be invited to, and acquaintances stopped calling her. "When I was just dating, when I wasn't really involved, it was okay. I mean, I was still involved in the lesbian community and I was still accepted. And then when I got . . . involved with a man. And it looked real. Then weird stuff happened. Lots of weird stuff happened. I'd get invited someplace and he wouldn't. By lesbian friends. . . . And sometimes I went, sometimes I didn't, depending on how I felt. . . . I'd get invited to a party and he wouldn't. And then when they needed a man to do something, he'd get invited. [Finally] I said forget it. I'm not available. We're not available. You know. It was really bad."

Like Sally Zimmerman, she felt hurt that the lesbian community was so unsupportive. "I was very hurt and pissed off and thought, you know, I've been through this. When . . . I finally came out as a lesbian, I lost a lot of straight people. The same kind of shit happened. Here I am again, in [this city], being with a man.

And the same stuff's happening from the lesbian community." Other things were also happening in her life at the time. She was involved in a new business, and her mother was ill. "But it was just, you know, I lost the community I was in. . . . I had a certain community; it was going. And then I was losing a lot of other stuff, too. I lost a lot of stuff in my life at that time, so I didn't have the energy to deal with people. And I have carried some bitterness with me. And have never confronted certain people." Now, she says, "It's such a relief not to care" about sexual identities and what other people think about her sexuality.

Unlabelled Identity

There are surely other bisexual identity accounts, both within this community and elsewhere. Many felt that bisexuality entails a freedom from identity and an ability to be much more fluid about sexuality than either lesbians or heterosexuals experience. Perhaps the most common bisexual acount is an *anti*-identity account. That is, for a number of women, what was important was not taking on a label and an identity but having the freedom to define themselves and live their lives as they please. Even those who proudly declared a bisexual identity tolerated much greater ambiguity around sexuality and a willingness to remain unlabeled, unidentified. Jan Liebow, for instance, a white woman who began acknowledging her feelings for both women and men after she became sober, said, "My sexuality is so much in the moment that I think that's why I have trouble describing it." She thinks of her sexuality as "evolving." "For me, in my life, there is so little love in this world and so relatively few opportunities to connect with people" that she hesitates to "restrict myself in some way, potentially closing myself to that possibility of connection, intimate connection and closeness with another being."

This flexibility may in part result from bisexuality's relative lack of institutionalization. Without established ways of "being" bisexual, bisexual women forge their own individual sexualities and may be freer to develop relationships unbound by stereotypes. At the same time, the freedom to establish new patterns may be accompanied by isolation. While shared norms and social institutions can restrict, they can also provide a camaraderie, a sense of shared purpose and commitment (Friedman and McAdam 1992).

The Elusiveness of Bisexual Community

If bisexuality is "everywhere and nowhere," as Marjorie Garber (1995) argues in her recent book, then in this community bisexual experience is everywhere and bisexual community, nowhere. Between 1989 and 1994, there was a flurry of activity, the beginnings of a nascent bi community, and then it disappeared. By 1994, "everyone" was talking about transgender issues, and bisexuality as an issue seemed to have disappeared—at least as it seemed to some bisexual women in the community.

For a brief period in the early 1990s there was a group called the Bi-Weekly Bi's. As Laurel Jameson recalled, that group formed out of a support group for bisexual women that had been meeting on campus. Before she located this group, Laurel had attempted to go to another support group, a mixed group for lesbians and bisexuals where, she says, "I got bi-phobia like you wouldn't believe. We're AIDS carriers, we're indecisive, we break people's hearts. . . . All the negative stereotypes were dumped all over me. And I remember just creeping away feeling really, really crappy." But at that group she was told about another bisexual support group. Although the group was primarily for young people on campus, "I went over there and hung out. . . . Here I am, I'm old enough to be everybody's mother or more. But it was good to be in a place where it was okay. . . . And realizing, okay, there's others of us out there. Lots of us."

When one of the women in that support group graduated, the group began to lose energy. After that, a couple of women decided to meet downtown, and thus began the Bi-Weekly Bi's. Every other week the group would meet at someone's house. "We had the best potluck suppers," Laurel recalled. "We ate and we hugged and we talked and we hung out. It was grand." The Bi-weekly Bi's didn't last, however. According to Laurel, two of the women in it had a feud, and when one attended, the other would not. After a while, when one of the main organizers moved out of town, the group stopped meeting.

During this time, several bisexual women, including Laurel, were actively trying to create greater visibility for bisexuals within the lesbian and gay community. After one bisexual woman had been "trashed" for her bisexuality at a Task Force work group, three bi activists wrote an open letter. Although they had long been active in the queer community—either as openly bisexual or "passing" as lesbian—they found bisexual activism and issues invisible and unacknowledged. Bisexuals were not included in the name of the Task Force, nor were their contributions recognized. In their letter, the women called on the Task Force to rectify the situation. This letter, Laurel recalled, was the catalyst for a meeting at which the name of the Task Force was broadened to include bisexuals.

Despite these efforts, bisexual community seemed elusive. Shortly after the Task Force changed its name, two of the women who had been most active in creating a bisexual presence in the community moved out of town. Although Laurel had been a catalyst, she said, "I'm not an organizer. I'm tired. I'm burned. And so we just let things fall by the wayside. . . . These days, I'm putting more energy into friends than into groups."

Others, who were not involved with either of these efforts, felt little support among bisexuals. Sally Zimmerman knew about the Bi-Weekly Bi's, but felt "they were women that I didn't really relate to." Like Judy Clausner, she sees little bisexual community, except for maybe a student support group. As she articulated it, the problem is the lack of numbers. There are simply too few open bisexuals to make a real community. "And I really miss that. I think I would really thrive and be really happy and contributing . . . to a larger group." These days, she looks to the broader progressive community for support.

Alex Goldman also sees little evidence of bisexual community. In 1994, she had recently visited Berkeley where "there was a strong bisexual community." Yet at home, she thinks there is actually more support for transgender issues than there is for bisexuals, a feeling Sally Zimmerman shares. "Somehow we skipped over, even though bisexual-the-name got included in all the labels, it sure seems like we jumped right over it."

Others saw little need for bi community. Cheryl Cook said, "It's my personality that I'm not a joiner. I try to envision, if I join such a group, what would I gain there, talking about—you know what I'm saying? Because I think a lot of the people have problems with their sexuality and accepting their sexuality. And I think those groups are wonderful. I don't have a problem with it, so I don't know what I would talk about. Maybe I'd meet more people, but I hesitate to meet people through my sexuality."

Judy Clausner is decidedly unenthusiastic about the prospects of creating another community with rules and regulations. Like Sally Zimmerman, she feels more connected to those in the broader progressive community who are doing antiracist work.

Strangers in a Common Land: Bisexuals in a Lesbian Community

Some are creating a place for bisexual women within the lesbian community. As the open letter to the Task Force pointed out, bisexuals have made many contributions to the lesbian and gay community—only they have not been recognized as openly bi. Laurel makes a distinction between bisexuals who live in the city, who identify with the lesbian and gay community, and those who live in the country just outside of town. Most "citified bi people, we're identified with the gay community. As far as I know. If we identify at all." "The country," she says, "is quite another matter. . . . You're going to reach out and find that country people are very different from urban gay people. You're gonna find they don't wear pink triangles, they don't organize for [antidiscrimination legislation]; you're going to find that they have a very different role with their family. You're going to find a lot of bisexuality; you're going to find girls who love each other and have sex with each other who are very married."

Although some of the bisexual women, like Laurel and Pat Lawler, feel lesbian-identified and fairly comfortable within the lesbian community, others, especially those who are involved with men, feel apart. Bisexuals who used to think of themselves as lesbian may have the hardest time carving out a niche for themselves within the community. Once she became involved with a man, for example, Sally Zimmerman felt very isolated. "I really feel much more like I have friends in the community, more than I feel a part of the community." She feels bisexuality incorporates the complexities of her identity and in that sense "being bisexual certainly is a very comfortable place to be." Yet, she said, "I don't think anybody really trusts me." Part of her is "furious" at the lesbian community and its lack of acceptance of her relationship with a man. "I thought, you people know what this is all about, and you should be making it easier for me. Because you know what it is to really live who you are, in a way that you really need to live it."

Alex's experience was similar. When she was involved with a man, she felt very isolated and distant from the lesbian community. But when she was involved with a woman, she felt "welcomed back into the fold." At the same time, she was skeptical: "It does seem to me that the acceptance of bisexuality is way more grudging than the acceptance of transgender." Ultimately, she thinks,

"It's who you sleep with that really is important. Not anything else. And bisexuals are not going to be accepted because they're sleeping with men."

Some lesbians are clearly hostile to bisexual women, especially those who are involved with men. But the detachment is not one-sided. As Sally noted, when she got married she withdrew. "I know that some of my limited involvement with the community right now is my own doing. It's very hard to live in two places at the same time. It is, and I think I have some pain about having had to choose."

When Laurel became reinvolved with her ex-husband, she, too, began to withdraw. "I've been trying to be sensitive to the fact that a lot of people don't want you running a man on them. . . . I still feel a responsibility to be sensitive and aware of people's feelings." But friends have not rejected her, and several have pressed her not to withdraw. Although she doesn't have time now to become involved in the Task Force leadership, she would like to become more active again and thinks, "I can be there and be bisexual." Perhaps because Laurel has always been known as bisexual she experiences more acceptance from others. "The people I know don't give me a hard time. We know each other, and they know where I'm coming from. And I've never lied about being bi. I've never made a pretense of something, so there was no surprise."

"Why I'm Not Bisexual"

As Paula Rust (1992a) has recognized, lesbian and bisexual women often lay claim to the same experience, yet interpret that experience differently. In her survey of 356 lesbian- and bisexual-identified women, both groups tended to have had sexual relationships with men, often significant ones. But women who thought of themselves as lesbians tended to interpret any relationship with a woman as evidence of a lesbian identity; bisexuals were more likely to incorporate both sets of experiences and attractions into their sexual identities. Rust argues that for lesbians, current *behavior* is of greater importance in signifying a lesbian identity, while for bisexuals, *feelings* of sexual attraction are more important. Although the lesbians in her survey may have permitted themselves to feel sexually attracted to men, as long as they did not act on them those feelings had little impact on their identities as lesbians. As Rust summed it up, "the maintenance of lesbian identity demands behavioral, but not emotional, exclusivity" (Rust 1992a, p. 380).

Most of the lesbians I interviewed had had relationships with men in the past. Although many of these relationships were casual or served only to confirm to the women that they were not, in fact, attracted to men,[3] some of the relationships were long-standing ones, including women who had been married for ten or twenty years. Only one of the women interviewed, Wendy Hammond, had never had even a casual relationship with a man.

This does not mean that all lesbians' relationships with men are important or reflective of a "true" bisexual identity—to suggest this would essentialize bisexual identity and discount lesbians' subjective senses of their own identities. The near ubiquitousness of relationships with men may simply reflect the compulsory heterosexuality to which most girls and women are subjected. But lesbians' and bisexuals' experiences do overlap. What is interesting are the ways in which lesbians and bisexuals differently interpret their experiences.

Several lesbians said that they sometimes were attracted to men; but they didn't think they would necessarily act on these attractions and they didn't feel the attractions had any bearing on their lesbian sexuality. Leslie Mohr said that for her, being a lesbian means "I don't ever want people to be able to assume that I'm straight. . . . I want people to assume that my most important relationships are with women, and that my love relationships and my sex relationships are with women . . . even if that's not exactly what might be going on." Leslie had had two relationships with men prior to coming out as a lesbian. She did not want to pretend that they hadn't happened or were somehow evidence of a false consciousness. "I was in love with these two particular men that I was in love with, and they were relationships that I was serious about and that I felt good about being in. . . . I never did really dismiss those relationships. I would say I was straight and now I'm a lesbian, but then, also, I . . . felt like I needed some way to account for the fact that I still sometimes am attracted to men."

Leslie's feelings coexist with an expansive definition of lesbianism. A good friend of hers is a "formerly lesbian" bisexual, but she does not see bisexuality as attractive for herself. She asks, "What can you do about desire? You just feel it. But I'm not very interested in getting involved with a man. That doesn't seem attractive to me—the kind of social aspects of that. But sometimes I feel sexually drawn to men that I know and sometimes have fantasies about having sex with a man. And I wonder if I will sometime, maybe, get involved with a man, although I don't want to now."

Marcela Reyes, too, admits that she still finds some men attractive. Unlike Leslie, she interprets her earlier experiences with men as "a bisexual phase, when I could not bear to admit that I would be a lesbian." Although she thought at the time that she "truly" was bisexual, she now sees herself as exclusively lesbian, a dyke. At the same time, she says, "I have to admit I still look at guys, but there's nothing really there. I'm attracted to physique. And I think that's okay for lesbians to do. I think some lesbians don't like that, or don't think that's a real lesbian, but I've broadened my scope of what a lesbian is." For both Marcela and Leslie, then, lesbian identity can include (and occlude) bisexuality.

Other lesbians suggested that in a different society, if relations between men and women weren't so oppressive, they might be bisexual. But given the current constellations of power, relationships with men are decidedly unattractive. Kate Foster no longer sees relationships with men as even a remote possibility. But in thinking over her history, she said, "I had some encounters with men that made me believe that in a different society I would perhaps be bisexual. There was no doubt in my mind that I was predominantly attracted to women." But, "at this point in my life, . . . my lesbian identity is absolutely clear. It's as much a part of me as having brown eyes."

Perhaps more typically, many of the lesbians interpreted their earlier experiences with men as a bisexual "phase": a period of exploration in which they dared not make the leap to lesbianism, or a time of immaturity or unwillingness to give up heterosexual privilege. Patrice Amaro said, "I identified as a bisexual person for about a year before actually identifying as a lesbian. . . . I ended up being involved with a man and a woman at the same time. And so purely by definition I ended up bisexual, only to find that I wasn't really—that once I met people who identified as lesbian, I realized that I felt much more accepted and much more nurtured in the lesbian community than I [did] as a straight person. I didn't like the kinds of energy that men give to women."

When she first came out, Denny Slater was afraid of the stereotypes associated with lesbians so she identified herself as bisexual. "I think that it took me until I had an understanding of the responsibilities I had to myself, as far as my relationships with other women." Only then could she identify as lesbian. "I had to have a better sense of my own maturity and that I was committed to my sexuality. And it took me a long while to do that." During that time, she had a number of sexual relationships with men, but, she said, "until I really let go of that need of mine to have their approval and society's approval, I didn't say or identify myself as a lesbian."

Other lesbians, in effect, argue that true bisexuality doesn't exist. If one is with a man, they claim, then one is heterosexual. If one is with a woman, one is lesbian. Unless one is in more than one relationship at the same time, bisexuality—to them—does not make sense.

Given her earlier marriage and satisfying sexual experiences with men, Joan Borman has thought a great deal about bisexuality.

"Unless one is in multiple relationships . . . one is either with a man or with a woman. I can conceptualize being a being who could at least conceive of, and maybe even actualize, being with a man and being with a woman." But this is decidedly unattractive. "Emotionally, men just seem to me to be inferior creatures. Or creatures who can't possibly measure up to what I want emotionally. So they're not part of the playing field, as far as I'm concerned. . . . So the term bisexuality doesn't make any sense to me. It doesn't make any sense. . . . Because at any given time, one's a lesbian if one's in a relationship with a woman and one's straight if one's in a relationship with a man." The notion "that they *could be* in a relationship with somebody" is not important to Joan. "What they're doing at the present time is who they are."

Mary Louise O'Neil, a mother of several teenage children, had been married for over ten years. When her marriage broke up, she entered into a long-term relationship with a woman, with whom she was still living in 1994. Mary Louise felt vehemently that bisexuality was a kind of "cop out." Earlier, when married, she said she would not have characterized herself as heterosexual "because I always had attractions to women. So I never, I always tried to not categorize myself." When she began to come out, she first thought of herself as bisexual, and she went to the campus bisexual awareness group. "Which didn't fit, you know, but it was a first step." Becoming a lesbian was, for her, a "revelation." Now, she reacts very negatively to bisexuality. "I still have a problem with bisexuality. It's like, you can't make up your mind. Or you won't make up your mind. And I think labeling myself a lesbian, I have made a choice. This is my choice." Later, she sent me a letter explaining in more detail her thoughts about bisexuality. Like Joan, she considered "if a woman is bisexual, the inherent assumption is that she is expressing her sexuality with both women and men partners." This she thought dangerous "disease-wise," but was also "emotionally irresponsible." Although nonmonogamy might be normal for a person in her early twenties, she thought it "reflects instability and immaturity at other ages." At the same time, she argued that male-female relationships are inherently unequal, which affects the kinds of relationships she feels she can have with either straight women or bisexuals. For her, friendships between bisexuals and lesbians are loaded with the weight of gender inequality.

Not all lesbians were hostile toward bisexual women. Deb Smith said, "I think it's very heartening that this is happening, and I really take these people seriously." Not to take bisexual women's understandings of who they are at face value is disrespectful. "If they say, 'I'm a bisexual and it means this,' you can't say under your breath, 'oh, hmm, you just haven't met the right girl yet.' Or that you're just fence-sitting." As bisexuality becomes more acceptable, she thinks that more lesbians will have relationships with men. "At some point, in some future life, they're going to be heterosexual, you know. They may not say that now, or never be able to conceive themselves as that, but that might be the case."

Kate Williams recalled changes in her thinking about bisexuality, sparked by her domestic partnership with a bisexual woman. "For years I felt that bisexuality was just a way of not really taking a stand on either side. And that was my fear—feelings and fears. And then I finally realized that there are people who are clearly, and can be responsible about, being attracted to both genders. And they're not necessarily—'Well, if I can't get me a woman tonight I'll get me a man.' They're not necessarily that. That's not necessarily bisexuality." One of the ways in which she could become comfortable thinking about bisexuality was to see it as a sexual orientation. Bisexuals "clearly don't have any more control of their orientation than I do." At the same time, she said, "I really believe the majority of people are bisexual." At the two extreme positions (one of which she sees herself as occupying) are exclusive heterosexuals and exclusive lesbians and gays.

In one sense, the assumption of lesbian identity by those with substantial heterosexual experience serves to keep bisexuality hidden. Marjorie Garber (1995) and others who write about bisexual experience, like Paula Rust, question this concealment. For those lesbians with substantial heterosexual experience and attraction, they might argue, why not take into account sexual experience and attraction over the life course? Why conceal this "hidden" bisexuality? Why not assume a bisexual identity or claim this sexual fluidity?

There are a number of reasons why lesbians do not claim bisexuality. First, to assume the identity—in contrast to having bisexual experience over the life course—implies an openness to relationships with men that many of the lesbians interviewed simply do not have. Although for some sexual relationships with men were possible, they were not preferred or even probable. These women might, under certain circumstances, find themselves attracted to men, but they did not actively seek out these attractions and would not necessarily act on them. They do not find social relationships with men, laden as they are with gender inequality, at all appealing. Thinking of themselves as bisexual would entail a sexualizing of their relationships with men as well as an identity shift, which they would have little motivation to carry out.

At the same time, to think of themselves as bisexual would, as Alex Goldman put it in 1994, "honor my past, more than my future." Now that she is again involved with a woman, she feels somewhat uncomfortable presenting herself as a bisexual. "It would put in people's faces a past that doesn't seem as relevant as a future." At the same time, calling herself a lesbian "would erase the past. If I were involved with a man, I would be happy to call myself bisexual because it would kind of challenge the notion of heterosexuality." But now, "I don't see the point, politically," of emphasizing a bisexual orientation.

Indeterminate Identities

The experiences of bisexual women highlight the fluidity of sexuality and the possibilities for changes in sexuality over the life course. In a postmodern moment, in which all categories are called into question, bisexuality seems uniquely suited to challenge the dualisms with which we commonly conceive of sexuality: male versus female, heterosexual versus homosexual. As some bisexual writers and activists have recently pointed out, bisexuality has this potentiality (see, e.g., Rust 1992b). Or it may, instead, become institutionalized as yet a third sexual category: another orientation, akin to heterosexuality and homosexuality. Perhaps the "discovery" of bisexuality by the popular press foreshadows this trend.[4]

For now, the lack of institutionalization, of fixed and determinate labels, may be freeing. Yet this very indeterminacy may also be one of the sources of tension between bisexual and lesbian women. As long as we work within a model of identity politics, in which inclusion is based on membership in a defined community, bisexuals may be viewed as too free-floating to be reliable allies. In the short range, tensions are likely to persist between bisexuals and those lesbians who, having "made a choice" as Mary Louise O'Neil would say, are unable to conceive of living outside of identity. In the long range, lesbians and bisexuals alike need to reconsider our commonalities and differences. As part of this, we all need to revision our models of community and how we might conceive of both being in common and accepting our differences.

9

Beyond Identity and Community?

> Before it is an identity, lesbianism is a characteristic of
> many diverse people.
>
> SHANE PHELAN (1994, p. 148)

In a rapidly changing world, how useful are identities? In a very real sense, identities are coercive; they pin people down in both intended and unintended ways. As Bonita Brown found out when she entered into the lesbian community, she could not make sense of the links between being a vegetarian, wearing Birkenstock sandals, and being a lesbian. How did one thing, loving women, entail the others? But while she could reject these other things for herself, while she could choose to eat meat and eschew sandals, she could not expunge those meanings for others. In this way, identities are accompanied by a freight of social baggage, some of which—perhaps, for some women, *much* of which—may be undesired.

Refusing identity, too, allows a certain freedom. As we slide toward this postmodern moment, we might thus question the restrictions of identification. Some women who were open to relationships with both men and women felt freer, more able to respond, by being flexible about their identities. For them, sexuality was an evolving process, always changing. To take on an identity, even a relatively open and fluid one, felt restrictive. Sexuality, for them, was to be lived "in the moment." And although some lesbians criticized them for failing to "make a decision" or refusing to "take a stand," these women felt more wholly themselves when not identified.

But although some can live outside of identity, to insist that all women should do so is restrictive. If one of the "goals" of a postmodern politics is to provide social spaces for greater individual democracy and freedom, then to assume a uniform fluidity is equally as narrow and restrictive as enforcing a uniform essentialism. To assume that all women want their sexuality to be fluid, elusive, is unwarranted. For some, identities provide an anchor and stability that is welcomed—as well as a potential basis for political mobilization.

To attempt to live outside of identity is thus not a perfect solution. And even if it were, it is not a choice lesbians can make wholly on their own. Even if we resist identifications, others will surely identify us. In this time and place, for those women who desire other women, it is difficult to resist being labelled lesbian. The experiences of bisexual women, whom others call lesbian or heterosexual despite what they called themselves, is illustrative. If even supposed allies miss the importance of self-definition, then it is surely a mistake to assume that the vast majority of people who are indifferent, let alone those who are actively hostile, will name us in the ways that we prefer.

Despite some of the problems involved in identification and identity politics, then, we shouldn't simply discard identities as a useful construct. While "labels may be for jars," as Katie Goshen reminded, they also provide help in ordering and making sense of the world. While "being" a lesbian does not quite fit the diverse experiences and attractions I have felt over my own life course, it certainly comes closer than anything else I can think of. What we need to figure out somehow is a more flexible, provisional way of identification. Given the escalating attacks on lesbians, gays, and bisexuals throughout the 1990s, this is increasingly imperative.

Identities and Politics, Politics of Identities

Questions of identity are central to the recent social ferment around issues of sexuality. Although lesbians, gays, and bisexuals have made a number of social and political gains in the 1980s and 1990s—inclusion in civil rights statutes, passage of domestic partnership ordinances, greater representation in popular culture, and so forth—these gains have been forcefully attacked by a loose coalition of groups and individuals bundled under the rubric of the religious Right. The political debates hinge very much on questions of identity. On the one hand, lesbians, gays, and bisexuals have made claims for inclusion in the political process on the basis of identity—as people who "are" identifiably lesbian, gay, or bisexual. Much organizing around this issue, at both the local and national level, has focused on the strategy of demonstrating that "we" are a recognizable group, based on shared identity.

On the other hand, religious rightists argue for a behavioral understanding of lesbian and gay sexuality. No one should be protected from discrimination, they argue, for what they do in bed—especially when, in their eyes, the behavior is sinful. Sodomy, they point out, is in many states illegal. And by focusing on sexual behavior, religious right wingers claim that they can "love the sinner but hate the sin." In a perverse parallel to constructionist arguments, religious conservatives argue that sexual identities are flexible and that sexuality can change over the life course. In the face of these arguments, as Shane Phelan (1994) argues, deconstructive political strategies may be disastrous. While it may be true that to call oneself a lesbian is only a shorthand term, a fairly rough way of noting a shifting and diverse array of feelings and practices, to deny that one "is" a lesbian in the face of right wing persecution is a self-defeating strategy. To try to deconstruct the categories of sex and gender in the political arena, in the context of an electorate accustomed to thirty-second sound bites, is at best confusing. While in the context of an academic arena, deconstruction may be a way to try to capture the complexities of lesbian performances and an important theoretical tool, in a political context, it appears a return to the closet or a refusal to fight.[1]

How to resolve this dilemma is not immediately apparent. Identity claims based on biology or essence or other "true believer" accounts are certainly not the answer. A political strategy based on the notion that we are "born that way" and thus "can't help ourselves" is, in the long run, doomed to backfire. Implicit in these claims is the notion that same-sex desire is somehow faulty, second rate, a misfortune of birth that can only be accommodated, never celebrated or even preferred. Besides, the identity accounts of ordinary lesbians and bisexuals clearly show that biologistic, essentialist accounts of sexuality do not encompass the full range of identities and sexualities. And what should formerly lesbian bisexuals, like Sally Zimmerman, do in the political meantime: hide from public view? claim a deviant deviancy?

Perhaps we need, instead, to think of identities provisionally, to recognize their performative aspects. For the moment we might say, 'This is what I am; this is how I perform my own, particular lesbian identity. But nothing in my past performances mandates that I must always be this way.' This might be a postmodern identity: a sense of one's identity as provisional, in flux, but as real nonetheless. Leslie Mohr, in a number of respects, seemed to exemplify this type of stance. Leslie didn't hesitate to call herself a lesbian, but she also maintained that being a lesbian did not "assert an identity with a stable content." And Laurel Jameson's qualification—"I'm a lesbian if bisexuality is included"—shows a willingness to stretch the categories to fit her own proclivities.

"True believer" accounts seem at odds with this kind of flexibility. Although some people, like Sally Zimmerman, are able to maintain a variety of true believer accounts—and able to change them to fit new circumstances—most probably are not. By their nature, as Marjorie Garber (1995) maintains, conversion accounts are binary. Lesbian, but not heterosexual. Gay, but not straight. Either, but not both. An attitude of skepticism toward identity seems more useful—at least at this political moment. A greater flexibility around identities and identifications could go a long way toward breaching some of the gaps between lesbians and bisexuals, as well as provide a way to continue organizing in the face of a right wing movement that would prefer to abolish same-sex desire as either identity or experience.

Reconceiving Community

If we are serious about becoming more flexible about the nature of identities and identifications, then we need to reconceive the notion of community as well. If lesbian identities are created, in part, within the context of lesbian communities, then we need to reconsider notions of community as based on shared identity and values and think about how different social structures might create the kinds of provisional identifications I've suggested. While some communitarian scholars, in response to the stress and anonymity of mass society, have advocated a general return to some form of community life, I question the utility of this as either social policy or as a political strategy for lesbians and bisexuals. If women are only fully welcomed into a lesbian community because they go to women's music concerts, poetry readings, lectures, and other community events, because they seem in a direct and visible way "like" other lesbians, then a great many women are left out—

women of color, poor and working-class lesbians, bisexuals, and old lesbians chief among them.

Although the lesbian community presented here seemed to have moved beyond its worst excesses, communities still, by their nature, are exclusive. A return to (or continuation of) the kinds of policing that can go on in intentional communities is not a useful strategy for social change. The notion that we need to "belong" to a community to share a common political agenda or make common cause is a troublesome one—and not one to move us forward in the long run.

Given the ubiquity of community life—or, at least, the language of community to refer to any kind of shared goal or project—we need, instead, to rethink community. Instead of seeing communities as places in which people really "are" alike in some fundamental way, we may be better off acknowledging that lesbian communities are really overlapping friendship networks, and sometimes exclusive ones at that, with multiple centers and fuzzy boundaries. If we think of communities in this way, it may be more possible to create political alliances across those networks and boundaries. It is much easier to become an ally with someone who is a friend of a friend.

If we think of communities thus, then we can also think of mobilizing parts of networks at different times and for different purposes. The response of many lesbians in joining with gay men to mobilize around AIDS provide one example; the responses of lesbian activists in states threatened by anti-gay ballot measures (like Oregon and Colorado) provide another. Not all lesbians have felt it a priority to work on AIDS issues; but those who have made connections with gay men on this issue have made links that may at least be potentially activated later on, at other times, in other struggles. Others have taken the example of AIDS activists to mobilize around breast cancer and lesbian health issues. One set of responses, the activation of one part of the network, does not invalidate others. "Real" lesbians work on AIDS issues and on breast cancer and on antipoverty projects and on passing domestic partner legislation and on raising children and so on. Engaging in social and political actions with others creates new network links; in so doing, we stretch ourselves. In learning to work with others who are different, we learn new tools for social and political action.

Rather than attempting to make one uniform lesbian "home" or "community," then, we need to think more pragmatically in terms of concrete projects and strategies. Rather than assume that we must share a common vision and grand agenda before we can begin to act, we must recognize that commonalities are forged out of action. In this way, we can learn to avoid the endless wrangling over who is or is not invited in. We can begin to imagine not some future lesbian "nation," but a proliferation of lesbian—and bisexual—projects and possibilities.

Appendix

Methodology

Participants for this study were recruited using chain referral techniques, augmented by posting leaflets in the lesbian/gay bar, the women's bookstore, and several other locations. A recruitment flyer was mailed with the newsletter of the Lesbian, Gay, and Bisexual Task Force. I also actively recruited participants at Task Force meetings, private parties, softball games, and social events. Twenty-five women were initially interviewed in 1989. Subsequently, seventy-seven participants were recruited to participate in a survey and card-sorting project in 1990. Thirteen of the twenty-five original interviewees were contacted again in 1994, and an additional eighteen women were interviewed at that time (for a total of forty-three women and fifty-six interviews). I maintained informal contact with a number of women after I left the community in 1991.

The initial interviewees were selected, in part, for their location in the community; I actively sought out those who were seen by others as at the "center" and at the "margins" of community life. I also sought out women, with varying degrees of success, in "under-represented" categories: old women, bisexual women, working-class women, and women of color. In the second wave of interviews conducted in 1994, I was especially interested in locating bisexual women and women who played softball. The resulting sample should in no way be seen as a representative sample of lesbian and bisexual women. Rather, like most lesbian and gay research, the sample includes those who participate in lesbian and gay community life. Those who are most out and open about their sexuality often tend to be white, middle-class, and highly educated—especially in a college town such as this one.

Thus, most of the interviewees had high levels of education. At the time of their first interview (either 1989 or 1994), the interviewees ranged in age from twenty to fifty-four years (with a mean age of just under thirty-six years). Although most had completed a college degree or some graduate and professional school, a few had less than a college degree (five). Still, the respondents' incomes did not match their levels of education. Just under one third of the sample had an income of less than $15,000 per year, and 40 percent had incomes ranging from $15,000 to $30,000. Another one third had incomes over $30,000. Four of the interviewees were women of color (African American, Asian, Latina, and Native American); five were Jewish. Ten considered themselves bisexual (at least at one point in time); the rest were lesbian.

The seventy-seven participants in the 1990 survey were slightly more diverse. Fifteen were women of color; the rest white. Most had high levels of education, although a few had only a high school diploma or less than two years of college. Still, many more had come from families with relatively little education. As with the interviewees, their incomes did not match their relatively high levels of education. Over 40 percent of the survey participants earned less than $15,000. Just over a third earned between $15,000 and $30,000, and less than one fourth earned over $30,000. Twelve of the survey participants considered themselves bisexual; the rest were lesbian.

Notes

INTRODUCTION

1. A number of recent books have focused on or included substantial sections on bisexuality; see, for instance, Garber 1995; Rust 1995; Weinberg, Williams, and Pryor 1994; D'Augelli and Patterson 1995.

CHAPTER 2

1. In the public debates about homosexuality in the early 1990s, as I have argued, issues of choice are being recast. Like the radical lesbian feminists of the 1970s, religious Right leaders of the 1990s argue that homosexuality is a choice. But instead of seeing it as a positive choice, as a way to struggle against men's domination, they cast it as a morally wrong choice, which should not be afforded civil rights protection. In response, many gays have vociferously set forth the argument that homosexuality is inborn; they argue that gays and lesbians no more choose their sexual orientation than African Americans choose their race and ethnicity or women their gender. In fact, a small number of gay researchers, including Simon LeVay (1991), are earnestly attempting to prove a biological basis for homosexuality. This public debate is sometimes split by gender, with men more likely to claim

that they were "always" gay or born that way than women (Bell and Weinberg 1978).

2. I believe that there may have been a separatist contingent in the 1970s and, perhaps, in the early 1980s. Several women told me about attempts to create lesbian land trusts during that time. Others told me that the community had, in recent years, "loosened up" in this regard, which suggests to me the existence of an early separatist group.

CHAPTER 3

1. Shortly after I wrote this chapter, I encountered Marjorie Garber's discussion of conversion narratives, in which she convincingly argues that these narratives obscure the possibilities of bisexuality (1995, chapter 15). As she notes, "Conversion is, to use an overworked term, 'binary.' It draws a line. It is not interested in questioning the existence, or the moving nature, of the borderline" (p. 346).

2. For examples of lesbian coming-out narratives, see Stanley and Wolfe (1980). Bisexual identity accounts may also bear similarities; see, for example, Hutchins and Kaahumanu (1991).

3. Groups that attempt to convert gays into "ex-gays" using a mixture of coercion and Biblical exhortation are another exception. Yet for them, sexual fluidity is desirable only if it moves in one direction: from gay to straight. Many lesbian and gay activists are understandably concerned about discussions of sexual fluidity. If sexual identity is seen as changeable over the life course, then lesbians and gays may face pressure to "convert." My argument is not that individuals can change identities at will, but that for some individuals, sexual identity is more fluid than it is for others. While indeed some individuals do experience change over the life course, others do not, and even those who experience change may not do so wholly volitionally.

4. I define celibacy here as including those women who either define themselves in that way or who consciously choose not to be available for a sexual relationship with another person. Those women who are not in a relationship at one or both points in time but are open to sexual relationships, I do not consider celibate, unless they have self-consciously chosen such a label for themselves.

5. One of the strategies of the religious Right is to define lesbian and gay identity as, essentially, behavior and then to equate same-sex sexual behavior with a wide variety of perversions (necrophilia, pedophilia, and so forth; for an example, see the pseudoscientific work of Paul Cameron, whose pamphlets are published by the Family Research Institute in Washington, D.C.).

CHAPTER 4

1. The notion of performance is not new. In the 1950s and 1960s, Erving Goffman (1959, 1974) outlined a dramaturgical approach in sociology. Goffman sees individuals as acting out roles, with front and back stage areas, audiences, and casts of performers acting in ensemble. There are distinct differences between Butler's (1990, 1991) and Goffman's notion of performance. One crucial difference between the two is that Butler argues there is no separate identity apart from or underneath the performance. For Butler, the "I" is produced in the process of performance. Conversely, Goffman seems to indicate that there is a "true self" underlying the performance, thus inserting distance between the self and the role. The question of whether or not there is something like an empirically verifiable "true" self apart from the performance is not particularly important for the current purposes. It may well be that some individuals *feel* that some performances are more indicative of a "true" self than others.

2. Given that Louise no longer thinks of herself as lesbian, I wonder if she can still summon up those feelings, through dress, that she is "really" lesbian. Unfortunately, I did not follow up on this in my second interview.

3. In 1988, when I began interviewing in this community, very few would have called themselves queer; that term was somewhat more common in 1994 as a way to signify a sense of being outsiders looking in.

4. Although I do not have enough systematic evidence to say this with any confidence, it seems to me that bisexual women are coded as distinctly not butch. The spring 1992 issue of *Out/Look,* which features several articles on bisexuality, is instructive. On the cover is a picture of a plump fem woman, presumably bisexual, with long hair, tight

short dress and matching high heels, holding the arm of a presumably heterosexual man. The balloon, drawn cartoon style to indicate her thoughts, contains a series of exclamation points and question marks. Looking on is a slender, chicly butch woman, presumably lesbian, with shorter, spiked hair, dressed in a white dinner jacket and black tie.

CHAPTER 5

1. A university group for gay and lesbian students of color was sometimes active, depending on the year and semester. But in the downtown community, there were no formal groups over the entire span of the study.
2. Unfortunately, I was not able to interview those women. That I was only able to interview women who interacted more with white women and who thought of themselves as part of the lesbian community is not surprising. The lack of stories by other women of color leaves an important hole in this book.
3. For a discussion of lesbian cultures, see Jeffner Allen (1990). See also Verta Taylor and Leila Rupp's (1993) argument that contemporary lesbian communities serve to keep feminism alive during the current period of abeyance.

CHAPTER 6

1. Following the lead of participants, I refer to "the" lesbian community. However, as I explore below, I recognize the problems inherent in referring to lesbian community as if it were one unified whole.
2. Both Krieger's and Zita's positions reflect an early enthusiasm and may not characterize either scholars' current sentiments. Zita is careful to distinguish her current ideas about lesbians and lesbian identity from her earlier thinking (personal communication 1995). See her 1990 essay for more recent work.
3. Interestingly, lesbian feminists and those who came out in the context of the feminist movement are increasingly being seen as the "old gays," in contrast to young lesbians, many of whom ally with direct action groups such as Lesbian Avengers and Act Up (Whisman 1991)

or what Arlene Stein (1992a) has referred to as "lifestyle lesbianism." See Arlene Stein (1993) and Robin Stevens (1994) for writings by and about the "newest" generation of lesbians.

4. By 1994, the group of women involved in sobriety programs seemed somewhat smaller (though still large relative to other groups). Ilene Zemke guessed that although many women were still involved, by 1994, women were not "coming new to it." She estimated that twelve-step programs peaked in popularity from about 1989 to about 1993.

5. I used "snowball" (or chain referral) sampling methods, augmented by recruitment at lesbian and gay events and meetings, and by posting fliers in a number of places frequented by lesbians. To avoid surveying people in only one or two friendship circles, I consciously sought out women in underrepresented categories. The survey sample is predominantly young (under age fifty) and well-educated. Fifteen of the survey respondents are women of color, and eleven are bisexual.

6. Defining who is a lesbian has been a preoccupation of many contemporary lesbians. See, for example, Ferguson (1981), Zita (1981), and Addelson's (1981) debate of Rich's notion of a lesbian continuum (1980). For a more recent sociological discussion, see Whisman (1993).

7. Identifying "core" members of the community is clearly a judgment call. I counted individuals as "core" when they were a leader of an organized social or political group, or when others considered them so. Sometimes, on hearing that I was studying the lesbian community, women would tell me that I should really speak to a particular woman because she was very active in the community.

CHAPTER 7

1. I myself, while conducting interviews about community norms, often wore short hair, slacks, and Birkenstock sandals and looked fairly androgynous. The point is not that women who conform are somehow weak or dupes, but that choices around style and appearance are not wholly personal or idiosyncratic.

2. I do not refer here to conservative critics' censure of feminist and lesbian political agendas but instead to the lively debates carried out among lesbians, bisexuals, and feminists.

3. See also the literature on merging and loss of self in lesbian couples; for example, Vargo (1987).

4. See also Tarrow's (1994) argument that cliques and factions are likely to develop in homogeneous groups.

CHAPTER 8

1. I did not interview any "swingers," who came to bisexuality through what Weinberg, Williams, and Pryor (1994) called the "sexual underground." In their study of San Francisco bisexuals, using data gathered from the 1980s, many saw their same-sex attractions as "added on" to heterosexuality. None of the women interviewed for this study came to bisexuality in that way.

2. Unfortunately, Chrissy could not be located for a reinterview in 1994.

3. After her eleven-year relationship with another woman broke up, for example, Susan Becker had a brief relationship with a man. After the first time she spent the night with him, she said, she was "convinced that I was, indeed, a lesbian."

4. Perhaps I should say "rediscovery." As Garber (1995, pp. 18–19) points out, *Time* and *Newsweek* both "discovered" bisexual chic in 1974 and, shortly thereafter, seemed to forget about it.

CHAPTER 9

1. For this reason, my students are often puzzled and dismayed by discussions of social constructionism. Lesbian students (and their allies) think that I mean that lesbian identities can be turned on and off at will, and that lesbians could somehow choose to be something different ("normal," "straight")—which is not at all how I intend it. Conservative students are similarly dismayed by my attempts to challenge the assumption of heterosexuality as natural and normal.

References

Addelson, Kathryn Pyne. 1981. "Words and Lives." *Signs* 7, pp. 187–99.

Allen, Jeffner, ed. 1990. *Lesbian Philosophies and Cultures*. Albany: State University of New York Press.

Anderson, Benedict. 1983. *Imagined Communities: Reflections on the Origin and Spread of Nationalism*. London: Verso.

Baetz, Ruth. 1980. *Lesbian Crossroads*. New York: William Morrow.

Barnhart, Elizabeth. 1975. "Friends and Lovers in a Lesbian Counterculture Community." Pp. 90–115 in Nona Glazier-Malbin, ed., *Old Family/New Family*. New York: Van Nostrand.

Bell, Alan P., and Martin S. Weinberg. 1978. *Homosexualities: A Study of Diversity among Men and Women*. New York: Simon and Schuster.

Bell, Alan P., Martin S. Weinberg, and Sue Kiefer Hammersmith. 1981. *Sexual Preference: Its Development in Men and Women*. Bloomington: Indiana University Press.

Bernard, Jessie. 1973. *The Sociology of Community*. Glenview, Ill.: Scott, Foresman.

Boswell, John. 1992. "Concepts, Experience, and Sexuality." Pp. 133–73 in Edward Stein, ed., *Forms of Desire: Sexual Orientation and the Social Constructionist Controversy*. New York: Routledge.

Bourdieu, Pierre. 1984. *Distinction: A Social Critique of the Production of Taste*. Cambridge, Mass.: Harvard University Press.

Buechler, Steven. 1990. *Women's Movements in the United States: Woman Suffrage, Equal Rights, and Beyond*. New Brunswick, N.J.: Rutgers University Press.

Burke, Peter, and Stephen L. Franzoi. 1988. "Studying Situations and Identities Using Experiential Sampling Methodology." *American Sociological Review* 53, pp. 559–68.

Burke, Peter, and Judy Tully. 1977. "The Measurement of Role Identity." *Social Forces* 55, 881–97.

Butler, Judith. 1990. *Gender Trouble: Feminism and the Subversion of Identity*. New York: Routledge.

————. 1991. "Imitation and Gender Insubordination." Pp. 13–31 in Diana Fuss, ed., *Inside/Out: Lesbian Theories, Gay Theories*. New York: Routledge.

Cartledge, Sue. 1980. "Bringing It All Back Home: Lesbian Feminist Morality." Pp. 93–103 in Gay Left Collective, ed., *Homosexuality: Power and Politics*. London: Allison and Busby.

Cass, Vivienne C. 1979. "Homosexual Identity Formation: A Theoretical Model." *Journal of Homosexuality* 4, pp. 219–35.

————. 1983/1984. "Homosexual Identity: A Concept in Need of Definition." *Journal of Homosexuality* 9, pp. 105–26.

Coleman, Eli. 1982. "Developmental Stages of the Coming-Out Process." Pp. 149–58 in William Paul, James D. Weinrich, John C. Gonsiorek, and Mary E. Hotvedt, eds., *Homosexuality: Social, Psychological, and Biological Issues*. Beverly Hills: Sage.

Combahee River Collective. 1977, reprinted 1981. "A Black Feminist Statement." Pp. 210–18 in Cherríe Moraga and Gloria Anzaldúa, eds., *This Bridge Called My Back: Writings by Radical Women of Color*. Watertown, Mass.: Persephone Press.

Coyle, Adrian. 1992. "'My Own Special Creation?' The Construction of Gay Identity." Pp. 187–220 in Glynnis M. Breakwell, ed., *Social Psychology of Identity and the Self Concept*. London: Surrey University Press.

D'Augelli, Anthony, and Charlotte J. Patterson. 1995. *Lesbian, Gay, and Bisexual Identities over the Lifespan: Gay and Bisexual Perspectives*. New York: Oxford University Press.

Davis, Madeline, and Elizabeth Lapovsky Kennedy. 1986. "Oral History and the Study of Sexuality in the Lesbian Community: Buffalo, New York, 1940–1960." *Feminist Studies* 12, pp. 9–26.

de Lauretis, Teresa, ed. 1991. *Queer Theory*. Special edition of *differences* 3.

D'Emilio, John. 1983. "Capitalism and Gay Identity." Pp. 100–113 in Ann Snitow, Christine Stansell, and Sharon Thompson, eds., *Powers of Desire: The Politics of Sexuality*. New York: Monthly Review Press.

D'Emilio, John, and Estelle Freedman. 1988. *Intimate Matters: A History of Sexuality in America*. New York: Harper and Row.

di Leonardo, Micaela. 1984. *The Varieties of Ethnic Experience: Kinship, Class, and Gender among Californian Italian-Americans*. Ithaca, N.Y.: Cornell University Press.

Dimen, Muriel. 1984. "Politically Correct? Politically Incorrect?" Pp. 138–48 in Carole S. Vance, ed., *Pleasure and Danger: Exploring Female Sexuality*. Boston: Routledge and Kegan Paul.

Epstein, Steven. 1987. "Gay Politics, Ethnic Identity: The Limits of Social Constructionism." *Socialist Review* 93/94, pp. 9–54. Reprinted as pp. 239–93 in Edward Stein, ed., *Forms of Desire: Sexual Orientation and the Social Constructionist Controversy*. New York: Routledge, 1992.

Espín, Oliva. 1987. "Issues of Identity in the Psychology of Latina Lesbians." Pp. 35–55 in Boston Lesbian Psychologies Collective, ed., *Lesbian Psychologies: Explorations and Challenges*. Urbana: University of Illinois Press.

Esterberg, Kristin. 1995. "Gay Cultures, Gay Communities: The Social Organization of Lesbians, Gay Men, and Bisexuals." Pp. 377–92 in Ritch C. Savin-Williams and Kenneth M. Cohen, eds., *The Lives of Lesbians, Gays, and Bisexuals: Developmental, Clinical, and Cultural Issues*. Fort Worth, Tex.: Harcourt Brace.

Faderman, Lillian. 1981. *Surpassing the Love of Men: Romantic Friendship and Love between Women from the Renaissance to the Present*. New York: Morrow.

———. 1985. "The 'New Gay' Lesbians." *Journal of Homosexuality* 10, pp. 65–75.

———. 1991. *Odd Girls and Twilight Lovers: A History of Lesbian Life in Twentieth-Century America*. New York: Columbia University Press.

Feinberg, Leslie. 1993. *Stone Butch Blues*. Ithaca, N.Y.: Firebrand.

Ferguson, Ann. 1981. "Patriarchy, Sexual Identity, and the Sexual Revolution." *Signs* 7, pp. 158–72.

Foucault, Michel. 1976 (reprinted 1980). *The History of Sexuality, Volume 1: An Introduction*. New York: Vintage.

Franchild, Edwina. 1990. "'You Do So Well': A Blind Lesbian Responds to Her Sighted Sisters." Pp. 181–91 in Jeffner Allen, ed., *Lesbian Philosophies and Cultures*. Albany: State University of New York Press.

Friedman, Debra, and Doug McAdam. 1992. "Collective Identity and Activism: Networks, Choices, and the Life of a Social Movement." Pp. 156–73 in Aldon D. Morris and Carol McClurg Mueller, eds., *Frontiers in Social Movement Theory*. New Haven: Yale University Press.

Fuss, Diana, ed. 1991. *Inside/Out: Lesbian Theories, Gay Theories*. New York: Routledge.

Garber, Marjorie B. 1995. *Vice Versa: Bisexuality and the Eroticism of Everyday Life*. New York: Simon and Schuster.

Gleason, Philip. 1983. "Identifying Identity: A Semantic History." *Journal of American History* 69, pp. 910–31.

Goffman, Erving. 1959. *The Presentation of Self in Everyday Life*. New York: Doubleday.

————. 1963. *Stigma: Notes on the Management of Spoiled Identity*. New York: Simon and Schuster.

————. 1974 (reprinted 1986). *Frame Analysis*. Boston: Northeastern University Press.

Golden, Carla. 1987. "Diversity and Variability in Women's Sexual Identities." Pp. 18–34 in Boston Lesbian Psychologies Collective, ed., *Lesbian Psychologies: Explorations and Challenges*. Urbana: University of Illinois Press.

————. 1994. "Our Politics and Choices: The Feminist Movement and Sexual Orientation." Pp. 54–70 in Beverly Greene and Gregory Herek, eds., *Lesbian and Gay Psychology: Theory, Research, and Clinical Applications*. Thousand Oaks, Cal.: Sage.

Gonsiorek, John C., and James R. Rudolph. 1991. "Homosexual Identity: Coming Out and Other Developmental Events." Pp. 161–76 in John C. Gonsiorek and James D. Weinrich, eds., *Homosexuality: Research Implications for Public Policy*. Newbury Park, Cal.: Sage.

Griggers, Cathy. 1993. "Lesbian Bodies in the Age of (Post)Mechanical Reproduction." Pp. 178–92 in *Fear of a Queer Planet: Queer Politics and Social Theory*. Minneapolis: University of Minnesota Press.

Hall, John R. 1992. "The Capital(s) of Cultures: A Nonholistic Approach to Status Situations, Class, Gender, and Ethnicity." Pp. 257–85 in Michèle Lamont and Marcel Fournier, eds., *Cultivating Differences: Symbolic Boundaries and the Making of Inequality*. Chicago: University of Chicago Press.

Hall, Stuart. 1989. "Ethnicity: Identity and Difference." *Radical America* 23, pp. 9–20.

Hoagland, Sarah Lucia. 1988. *Lesbian Ethics*. Palo Alto, Cal.: Institute of Lesbian Studies.

Hoagland, Sarah Lucia, and Julia Penelope, eds. 1988. *For Lesbians Only: A Separatist Anthology*. London: Onlywomen Press.

Hutchins, Loraine, and Lani Kaahumanu. 1991. *Bi Any Other Name: Bisexual People Speak Out*. Boston: Alyson.

Jenness, Valerie. 1992. "Coming Out: Lesbian Identities and the Categorization Problem." Pp. 65–74 in Ken Plummer, ed., *Modern Homosexualities: Fragments of Lesbian and Gay Experience*. London: Routledge.

Kaufman, H. F. 1966. "Toward an Interactional Conception of Community." In Roland Warren, ed., *Perspectives on the American Community*. Chicago: Rand McNally.

Kennedy, Elizabeth Lapovsky, and Madeline Davis. 1993. *Boots of Leather, Slippers of Gold: The History of a Lesbian Community*. New York: Routledge.

Kirk, Marshall, and Hunter Madsen. 1989. *After the Ball: How America Will Conquer Its Fear and Hatred of Gays in the 90s*. New York: Plume.

Kitzinger, Celia. 1987. *The Social Construction of Lesbianism*. London: Sage.

Kitzinger, Celia, and Rachel Perkins. 1993. *Changing Our Minds: Lesbian Feminism and Psychology*. New York: New York University Press.

Klein, Fritz. 1993. *The Bisexual Option*. New York: Haworth.

Krieger, Susan. 1982. "Lesbian Identity and Community: Recent Social Science Literature." *Signs* 8, pp. 91–108.

———. 1983. *The Mirror Dance: Identity in a Women's Community*. Philadelphia: Temple University Press.

LeVay, Simon. 1991. "A Difference in Hypothalamic Structure Between Heterosexual and Homosexual Men." *Science* 253, 1034–37.

Levine, Martin. 1992. "The Life and Death of Gay Clones." Pp. 68–86 in Gilbert Herdt, ed., *Gay Culture in America: Essays from the Field*. Boston: Beacon Press.

Lewis, Sasha G. 1979. *Sunday's Women: Lesbian Life Today*. Boston: Beacon Press.

Lockard, Denyse. 1985. "The Lesbian Community: An Anthropological Approach." *Journal of Homosexuality* 11, pp. 83–95.

Lorde, Audre. 1984. "Age, Race, Class, and Sex: Women Redefining the Difference." Pp. 114–23 in Audre Lorde, *Sister Outsider*. Trumansburg, N.Y.: Crossing Press.

Loulan, JoAnn. 1984. *Lesbian Sex*. San Francisco: Spinsters Ink.

———. 1987. *Lesbian Passion: Loving Ourselves and Each Other*. San Francisco: Spinsters/Aunt Lute.

McCowan, Lyndall. 1992. "Re-Collecting History, Renaming Lives: Femme Stigma and the Feminist Seventies and Eighties." Pp. 299–328 in Joan Nestle, ed., *The Persistent Desire: A Femme-Butch Reader*. Boston: Alyson.

McCoy, Sherry, and Maureen Hicks. 1979. "A Psychological Retrospective on Power in the Contemporary Lesbian-Feminist Community." *Frontiers* 4, pp. 65–69.

McIntosh, Mary. 1981. "The Homosexual Role." Pp. 30–49 in Kenneth Plummer, ed., *The Making of the Modern Homosexual*. Totawa, N.J.: Barnes and Noble.

McWhirter, David P., Stephanie A. Sanders, and June Machover Reinisch, eds. 1990. *Homosexuality/Heterosexuality: Concepts of Sexual Orientation*. New York: Oxford University Press.

Minton, H. L., and G. J. McDonald. 1983/1984. "Homosexual Identity Formation as a Developmental Process." *Journal of Homosexuality* 9, 91–104.

Moraga, Cheríe, and Gloria Anzaldúa. 1981. *This Bridge Called My Back: Writings by Radical Women of Color*. Watertown, Mass.: Persephone Press.

Murray, Steven O. 1979. "The Institutional Elaboration of a Quasi-Ethnic Community." *International Review of Modern Sociology* 9, pp. 165–77.

————. 1992. "Components of Gay Community in San Francisco." Pp. 107–46 in Gilbert Herdt, ed., *Gay Culture in America: Essays from the Field*. Boston: Beacon Press.

Near, Holly. 1990. *Fire in the Rain, Singer in the Storm*. New York: Morrow.

Nestle, Joan. 1987. *A Restricted Country*. Ithaca, N.Y.: Firebrand.

————, ed. 1992. *The Persistent Desire: A Femme-Butch Reader*. Boston: Alyson.

Newton, Esther. 1993. *Cherry Grove, Fire Island*. Boston: Beacon Press.

Phelan, Shane. 1989. *Identity Politics: Lesbian Feminism and the Limits of Community*. Philadelphia: Temple University Press.

————. 1993. "(Be)Coming Out: Lesbian Identity and Politics." *Signs* 18, pp. 765–90.

————. 1994. *Getting Specific: Postmodern Lesbian Politics*. Minneapolis: University of Minnesota Press.

Plummer, Kenneth. 1981. "Homosexual Categories: Some Research Problems in the Labelling Perspective of Homosexuality." Pp. 53–75 in Kenneth Plummer, ed., *The Making of the Modern Homosexual*. Totawa, N.J.: Barnes and Noble.

————, ed. 1992. *Modern Homosexualities: Fragments of Lesbian and Gay Experience*. N.Y.: Routledge.

Portes, Alejandro, and Robert Manning. 1986. "The Immigrant Enclave: Theory and Empirical Examples." Pp. 47–68 in Susan Olzak and Joane Nagel, eds., *Competitive Ethnic Relations*. Orlando, Fla.: Academic.

Pratt, Minnie Bruce. 1995. *S/he*. Ithaca, N. Y.: Firebrand.

Queen, Carol. 1992. "Strangers at Home: Bisexuals in the Queer Movement." *Out/Look* 16, pp. 23–33.

Radicalesbians. 1970 (reprinted 1988). "The Woman-Identified Woman." Pp. 17–22 in Sarah Lucia Hoagland and Julia Penelope, eds., *For Lesbians Only: A Separatist Anthology*. London: Onlywomen Press.

Redstockings Manifesto. 1970. Pp. 533–36 in Robin Morgan, ed., *Sisterhood Is Powerful*. New York: Vintage.

Rich, Adrienne. 1980. "Compulsory Heterosexuality and Lesbian Existence." *Signs* 5, pp. 631–60.

Rosenberg, Morris. 1987. "Depersonalization: The Loss of Personal Identity." Pp. 193–206 in Terry Honess and Krysia Yardley, eds., *Self and*

Identity Perspectives across the Life Span. New York: Routledge and Kegan Paul.

Rust, Paula. 1992a. "The Politics of Sexual Identity: Sexual Attraction and Behavior among Lesbian and Bisexual Women." *Social Problems* 39, pp. 366–86.

———. 1992b. "Who Are We and Where Do We Go from Here? Conceptualizing Bisexuality." Pp. 281–310 in Elizabeth Reba Weise, ed., *Closer to Home: Bisexuality and Feminism*. Seattle, Wash.: Seal Press.

———. 1993. "'Coming Out' in the Age of Social Constructionism: Sexual Identity Formation among Lesbian and Bisexual Women." *Gender and Society* 7, pp. 50–77.

———. 1995. *Bisexuality and the Challenges to Lesbian Politics: Sex, Loyalty, and Revolution*. New York: New York University Press.

Seidman, Steven. 1993. "Identity and Politics in a 'Postmodern' Gay Culture: Some Historical and Conceptual Notes." Pp. 105–42 in Michael Warner, ed., *Fear of a Queer Planet: Queer Politics and Social Theory*. Minneapolis: University of Minnesota Press.

Simon, William, and John H. Gagnon. 1967. *Sexual Deviance*. New York: Harper and Row.

Smith-Lovin, Lynn, and David Heise. 1988. *Analyzing Social Interaction: Advances in Affect Control Theory*. London: Gordon and Breach.

Smith, Barbara, ed. 1983. *Home Girls: A Black Feminist Anthology*. New York: Kitchen Table Press.

Smith, Dorothy. 1987. *The Everyday World as Problematic*. Boston: Northeastern University Press.

Snitow, Ann, Christine Stansell, and Sharon Thompson, eds. 1983. *Powers of Desire: The Politics of Sexuality*. New York: Monthly Review Press.

Sophie, Joan. 1985/1986. "A Critical Examination of Stage Theories of Lesbian Identity Development." *Journal of Homosexuality* 12, 39–51.

Stanley, Julia Penelope, and Susan J. Wolfe. 1980. *The Coming Out Stories*. Watertown, Mass.: Persephone Press.

Stein, Arlene. 1992a. "All Dressed Up but No Place to Go? Style Wars and the New Lesbianism." Pp. 431–39 in Joan Nestle, ed., *The Persistent Desire: A Femme-Butch Reader*. Boston: Alyson.

———. 1992b. "Sisters and Queers: The Decentering of Lesbian Feminism." *Socialist Review* 22: 33–55.

————, ed. 1993. *Sisters, Sexperts, Queers: Beyond the Lesbian Nation*. New York: Plume.

Stein, Edward. 1992. *Forms of Desire: Sexual Orientation and the Social Constructionist Controversy*. New York: Routledge.

Stevens, Robin, ed. 1994. *Girlfriend Number One: Lesbian Life in the 90s*. Pittsburgh: Cleis.

Stryker, Sheldon. 1980. *Symbolic Interactionism*. Menlo Park, Cal.: Benjamin/Cummings.

————. 1987. "The Interplay of Affect and Identity: Exploring the Relationships of Social Structure, Social Interaction, Self, and Emotion." Paper presented at the annual meeting of the American Sociological Association, August 1987.

Tarrow, Sidney. 1994. *Power in Movement: Social Movements, Collective Action, and Politics*. Cambridge: Cambridge University Press.

Taylor, Verta, and Leila Rupp. 1993. "Women's Culture and Lesbian Feminist Activism: A Reconsideration of Cultural Feminism." *Signs* 19, pp. 32–61.

Taylor, Verta, and Nancy Whittier. 1992. "Collective Identity in Social Movement Communities: Lesbian Feminist Mobilization." Pp. 104–29 in Aldon D. Morris and Carol McClurg Mueller, eds., *Frontiers in Social Movement Theory*. New Haven, Conn.: Yale University Press.

Troiden, Richard. 1988. *Gay and Lesbian Identity: A Sociological Analysis*. Dix Hills, N.Y.: General Hall.

Vance, Carole, ed. 1984. *Pleasure and Danger: Exploring Female Sexuality*. New York: Routledge and Kegan Paul.

Vargo, Sue. 1987. "The Effects of Women's Socialization on Lesbian Couples." Pp. 161–73 in Boston Lesbian Psychologies Collective, ed., *Lesbian Psychologies: Explorations and Challenges*. Urbana: University of Illinois Press.

Warner, Michael, ed. 1993. *Fear of a Queer Planet: Queer Politics and Social Theory*. Minneapolis: University of Minnesota Press.

Waters, Mary. 1990. *Ethnic Options: Choosing Identities in America*. Berkeley: University of California Press.

Weeks, Jeffrey. 1981. "Discourse, Desire, and Sexual Deviance: Some Problems in a History of Homosexuality." Pp. 76–111 in Kenneth Plummer, ed., *The Making of the Modern Homosexual*. Totawa, N.J.: Barnes and Noble.

—————. 1987. "Questions of Identity." Pp. 31–51 in Pat Caplan, ed., *The Cultural Construction of Sexuality*. London: Tavistock.

Weinberg, Martin S., Colin J. Williams, and Douglas W. Pryor. 1994. *Dual Attraction: Understanding Bisexuality*. New York: Oxford University Press.

Weinberg, Thomas S. 1984. "Biology, Ideology, and the Reification of Developmental Stages in the Study of Homosexual Identities." *Journal of Homosexuality* 10, pp. 77–84.

Weinrich, James. 1992. "Reality or Social Construction?" Pp. 175–208 in Edward Stein, ed., *Forms of Desire: Sexual Orientation and the Social Constructionist Controversy*. New York: Routledge.

Weise, Elizabeth Reba, ed. 1992. *Closer to Home: Bisexuality and Feminism*. Seattle, Wash.: Seal Press.

West, Candace, and Sarah Fenstermaker. 1995. "Doing Difference." *Gender and Society* 9, pp. 8–37.

Weston, Kath. 1991. *Families We Choose: Lesbians, Gays, Kinship*. New York: Columbia University Press.

Whisman, Vera. 1991. "Different from Whom? Competing Definitions of Lesbianism." Paper presented at the annual meetings of the American Sociological Association, Cleveland, Ohio.

—————. 1993. "Identity Crises: Who Is a Lesbian Anyway?" Pp. 47–60 in Arlene Stein, ed., *Sisters, Sexperts, Queers: Beyond the Lesbian Nation*. New York: Plume.

—————. 1996. *Queer by Choice: Lesbians, Gay Men, and the Politics of Identity*. New York: Routledge.

Wolf, Deborah G. 1979. *The Lesbian Community*. Berkeley: University of California Press.

Zita, Jacquelyn. 1981. "Historical Amnesia and the Lesbian Continuum." *Signs* 7, pp. 172–87.

—————. 1990. "Lesbian Body Journeys: Desire Making Difference." Pp. 327–45 in Jeffner Allen, ed., *Lesbian Philosophies and Cultures*. Albany: State University of New York.

Index